Faith's Journey
Confronts Obstacles

Faith's Journey Confronts Obstacles

Instructing God's Soldiers
to Overcome in His Armor

R. C. JETTE

RESOURCE *Publications* • Eugene, Oregon

FAITH'S JOURNEY CONFRONTS OBSTACLES
Instructing God's Soldiers to Overcome in His Armor

Resource Publications
An Imprint of Wipf and Stock Publishers
199 W. 8th Ave., Suite 3
Eugene, OR 97401

www.wipfandstock.com

PAPERBACK ISBN: 978-1-5326-8189-9
HARDCOVER ISBN: 978-1-5326-8190-5
EBOOK ISBN: 978-1-5326-8191-2

Manufactured in the U.S.A.   APRIL 10, 2019

All Scripture quotations are taken from the KING JAMES VERSION (KJV): KING JAMES VERSION, public domain.

This book is dedicated to Jesus Christ who is the Author and Finisher of my faith, to Paul my husband and soul mate, to my three children, to my five grandchildren, and to all who have encouraged my life throughout the years.

A special heartfelt thanks is given to Wipf and Stock Publishers for making this all possible, for their professional staff who worked so charitably with me, and for previously publishing: *Storms Are Faith's Workout: Preparing Christians for Spiritual Ambush (2018); The Elfdins and the Gold Temple (2018); Charlie McGee and the Leprechaun (2019).*

Jesus said unto him, if thou canst believe,
all things are possible to him that believeth (Mark 9:23).

Contents

Introduction ix

Chapter 1: Obstacle—Faith's Birth 1

Chapter 2: Obstacle—Faith's Examination 10

Chapter 3: Obstacle—Faith's Armor 18

Chapter 4: Obstacle—Faith's Nemesis 28

Chapter 5: Obstacle—Faith's Love 35

Chapter 6: Obstacle—Faith's Purge 40

Chapter 7: Obstacle—Faith's Mind 47

Chapter 8: Obstacle—Faith's Foundation 53

Chapter 9: Obstacle—Faith's Freedom 59

Chapter 10: Obstacle—Faith's Rest 66

Chapter 11: Obstacle—Faith's Satisfaction 71

Chapter 12: Obstacle—Faith's Secret 79

Chapter 13: Obstacle—Faith's Impediment 87

Chapter 14: Obstacle—Faith's Journey 97

Introduction

WHEN THE LORD IMPRESSED me to begin writing at seventy-one years of age, I obeyed although I was all at sea. I knew the book was essential, because Christians are struggling with storms trying to overcome their faith and many are discouraged and downtrodden by the onslaught. However, when I finished my first book, *Storms Are Faith's Workout: Preparing Christians for Spiritual Ambush,* I did not think that I would write another book about faith. As a matter of fact, I started doing biblical based fiction. The two that are published by Wipf and Stock Publishers were done as allegories. *The Elfdins and the Gold Temple* is to reveal what happens to Christians that forget about God when doing spiritual warfare and revert to natural or physical means to defeat a supernatural enemy. *Charlie McGee and the Leprechaun* reveals a young man overwhelmed by an incredible storm and his quest to discover the truths of the Bible.

In this book, I feel the Lord wants to stress the truth that many Christians lack an understanding of faith's journey, how the soldiers of God are armored, and how to be prepared for spiritual warfare. He has shown me through my years of ministry that many times seeing things from a different perspective enables us to see what we did not see or understand previously. It seems that when something is seen in a different light, it becomes understandable. Although I will reveal many obstacles in this book, they are not meant to be an end. The hindrances revealed are to give insight into comprehending that we will confront many obstacles in faith's journey and they are probably perpetual.

This book is meant to encourage and enlighten all who read it with a knowledge to live an overcoming faith walk, with an understanding of God's supernatural armor, with an understanding that faith's journey will confront many obstacles, and that God's soldiers must be fully dressed in His armor if we are to overcome by faith.

It was revealed in *Storms Are Faith's Workout*, Christians will experience storms or trials of their faith. How we react during the storms of our life determines whether we overcome the storm, or the storm overcomes us. This book is meant to reveal how faith works and the necessity of the full armor of God. With the knowledge of God's armor, God's soldiers will be enabled to stand against any obstacle the devil puts in our path.

As stated in the previous book, storms are not probable in a Christian's life, they are sure and certain. We can expect storms as sure as we expect the sun to rise and set each day. This book reveals that faith's journey will confront obstacles as sure as the sun rises and sets each day. God's soldiers are ever in warfare. We may have times of refreshing, but this life is one of combat. There is no retiring from the army of the Lord until we are called home or Jesus returns.

Believe me, there are no shortcuts to overcoming in this life. Obstacles will come, and they will come unexpectedly, but they do not have to overwhelm us. We may get dazed, but we don't have to be devastated and feel hopeless. Faith in God is the bedrock that will keep us from getting uprooted no matter how violent the storm or how gigantic the obstacle. But as stated in my previous book, faith is only as strong as our love for God and belief in His love for us. This book will not bring forth the foundation from the first book but will build on the knowledge gained from *Storms Are Faith's Workout*. If you have not read it, this book will still help prepare and encourage you on your journey of faith.

However, if you have not read *Storms Are Faith's Workout*, I recommend that you read it. In it are scriptural and personal examples that will help enlighten God's love for you and how your faith must be rooted in His love. All that God does and allows in your life is done out of His great love for you. He has one desire for you and that is that you spend eternity with Him. As stated, this book will not deal with what was revealed in the first book, however, it may overlap in a few areas. *Faith's Journey Confronts Obstacles: Instructing God's Soldiers to Overcome in His Armor* is meant to give you a greater understanding that to overcome, you must confront many obstacles. These obstacles can only be confronted and overcome if you learn to use the whole armor of God. Without God's armor, we face an enemy that will utterly destroy us. Flesh and blood is no match against a supernatural spirit being.

Reader, I believe that the Holy Spirit led you to pick up this book, because you seem to be losing battles. You have tried and tried to overcome but haven't been able to do so. God wants you to know that He loves you and wants you to overcome more than you do. He has seen you go to battle after battle without His armor. Although you are familiar with it, you have not grasped that it is vital to your overcoming by faith. You don't fully dress in it, you are not sure how to use it, you are not sure of what it does, and you have not been standing against the enemy fully armed. But be of good cheer, this book is inspired by God to familiarize you with His armor. In its pages, you will learn how the full armor of God will help you to confront obstacles, how it will prepare you for spiritual warfare, and how you will be enabled to overcome by faith in His armor!

Chapter 1

Obstacle: Faith's Birth

For by grace are ye saved through faith; and that not of yourselves: it is the gift of God: Not of works, lest any man should boast (Ephesians 2:8–9).

WHY AM I DOING another book on faith? I know there are so many books out there about faith. However I believe the difference here is that it reveals that faith is not merely believing. It is being prepared for spiritual warfare and then confronting the obstacle by faith. To overcome by faith, God's soldiers must learn to confront all obstacles by standing in the full armor of God. As in *Storms Are Faith's Workout*, I will build a firm foundation. Therefore, we won't start to discuss God's armor until Chapter three.

In our society of instant this and instant that, Christians can be swayed into the mentality of not enduring or persisting until the obstacle is overcome. Faith is not always understood. Like I stated in my introduction, sometimes seeing things from a different perspective can illuminate what was not understood previously.

This book is to reveal that to succeed on faith's journey, we must first be prepared for spiritual warfare and then confront the obstacle by faith. All the obstacles in this book can be an obstacle because if not overcome by faith, they will hinder faith's journey.

The title of this chapter shows that the first obstacle on our journey is faith's birth. Without becoming born again, there is no faith journey. That's why we must understand the difference between believing and confronting. Without confronting, we will not overcome the first obstacle to salvation.

> Thou believest that there is one God; thou doest well: the devils also believe, and tremble (James 2:19).

There is a difference between believing and actual saving or victorious faith that has confronted an obstacle and has overcome it by faith. The devils believe, but they will never be saved. Their belief is not faith that will save them. The obstacle of faith's birth is one that many can relate to. I will give a few examples to reveal how it can be an obstacle. When my husband was coming to the Lord, he had to confront and overcome the lies thrown at him from the devil and people. He was told that if he left the Catholic Church he would burn in hell and that it was the only true church started by the Apostle Peter.

It didn't rest well with him that only one Christian Church was true. His heart felt that any denomination that believed in Jesus as Savior could not be wrong. Of course, he didn't know the Bible and that Jesus has one Body with many members. Anyway, he continued going to the Baptist Church and one morning he knew that he had to go to the altar. As he was walking down the aisle to accept Jesus as Savior, he had a peace that he was making the right decision. Now, if he had listened to the lies, he would not have walked down the aisle to accept Christ as his Savior. He has been saved and serving the Lord for thirty-six years.

My obstacle was one that took longer to confront and to overcome. When I was about thirteen or fourteen, I went to a Billy Graham Crusade and went to the altar. I remember crying, walking down the aisle, and then being in a room. In the room, a young lady told me to write the date in my Bible. She said that I needed to remember that date as the date that Jesus became my Savior. Although, I never wrote the date in a Bible, I was convinced that I was born again and held that as truth for many years. When I was

left alone with three children (ages 2, 4, and 5), no car, two mort-
gages, bills, and going through a divorce, I had a Baptist Minister
visit. He asked me if I was saved, and I told him about my experience at the crusade. He then asked me if I had been baptized in
water and I told him that I had not. He told me that water baptism
is the first act of obedience and that I must make a public profession of faith. Anyway, I was baptized in water, went down a dry
sinner, and came up a wet sinner. More years went by with me
thinking I was saved. One of my brothers tried to commit suicide
(not the one in Storms) and I was begging God for him to live. He
had a wife, four children, and one on the way.

My son had given me a hard time before the news about my
brother and heard me crying. He came to my room, knocked on
my door, and I had him come in. He said he was sorry for giving
me a hard time. I told him that I was not crying about that and
explained that his Uncle Frank tried to kill himself. I then told
him to go back to bed, that I loved him, and of course, I forgave
him. When he closed my door, I heard in my heart, "I love you, of
course, I forgive you." Then I really cried and said, "Jesus, it's you.
You've been here all the time. I never knew. I never knew." That
experience is one that I can remember every detail. My belief went
from head knowledge to a heart changing experience. Of course,
I was baptized in water after that and have been serving the Lord
and ministering for almost forty years.

That makes me wonder how many others have been living
such a defeated life and not experiencing the Lord's love and presence in their life because they are not really saved. I know that it
can happen, I lived it for about eighteen years. Have they had a
head salvation experience and not a heart changing experience?
I pray this book will help some to understand that believing is
not enough. That belief must be a heart changing experience that
changes our life. It will change our desires, our speech, our actions,
our thoughts, our beliefs, etc. to that which pleases God.

This book is to reveal what true faith in Jesus Christ can do. It
is a faith that will not only confront but overcome any obstacle the
devil throws at us. We cannot walk faith's journey and not expect

difficulties. By the time this book is finished, God's soldiers should understand that faith's journey includes obstacles that we must not only be prepared for, but that must be confronted by faith while being fully clothed in God's armor.

Okay, let's look at the word *faith*. According to Webster's dictionary, faith is a belief in what is declared by another. This means that we have faith in someone's testimony, or we have no faith in someone's testimony. Those of you who have read *Storms Are Faith's Workout* know the story of the Niagara Falls crowd that gave an understanding of what true faith is.

When we listen to someone speak or read their declaration, we either believe them or we disbelieve them. Faith either believes or doesn't believe what the person has declared. However, the belief is not superficial or head knowledge, which must be understood if salvation is to take place.

In Ephesians 2:8, faith means a persuasion, assurance, or conviction of the truthfulness of God. It is a belief and a trust in whatever God declares. It is believing His word. This believing is not a head knowledge, it is a heart changing belief in what God declares. It is being completely persuaded without any shadow of doubt that what God has said is truth. Merely believing something and being fully persuaded in that thing is at the opposite ends of the spectrum. It is the opposite of the devils believing and the believing of the child of God.

> Thy testimonies that thou has commanded are righteous
> and very faithful (Psalms 119:138).

The Psalmist believed God's testimonies, God's declarations, or God's word. In the scripture in Ephesians, we are told that we are saved by grace through faith and that is the gift of God. It is not of works, or we could boast.

The Greek word for *gift* in that scripture means a present (specifically a sacrifice), an offering. Now, we know that whatever God does for us is a gift. My question here is, does the gift refer to grace, salvation, or faith? Yet, the Greek word in that scripture for gift means a present or an offering (specifically a sacrifice).

I wouldn't call God's grace a sacrifice, nor would I call faith a sacrifice. A sacrifice is an expense, a disadvantage, a cost, a suffering, etc. Our salvation comes through Christ's sacrifice or suffering on the cross. His sacrificial death was God's gift to sinful man. For without Christ's suffering, there would be no salvation.

Yes, I know that God's grace is also a gift to us, but in Ephesians 2:8, the Greek word for *grace* refers to God's influence upon the heart of man to believe His testimony, His declaration, His word. But the word gift in Ephesians refers to a sacrifice. The grace or influence of the Holy Spirit moving on our heart is not a sacrifice, it is His influencing our heart to believe His declaration that what He has said in His word is truth.

> As it is written, There is none righteous, no, not one: There is none that understandeth, there is none that seeketh after God (Romans 3:10–11).

You see, God loves us so much that He keeps influencing our heart to get us to respond. Without Him coming after us, we would never understand His word and we would never seek after Him. It is His grace that is ever working to influence our heart to cause us to believe His word and act upon that influence.

What we must understand is that grace is the influence that enables us to believe and faith is the act of believing. We must act upon the influence of grace. If we reject (as multitudes do), then God's grace or influence which enables us to believe God can never birth the faith that saves. That's why the first obstacle in faith's journey is faith's birth. If we do not act upon that influence, we will never begin our journey of faith.

> Jesus answered and said unto him, Verily, verily, I say unto thee, Except a man be born again, he cannot see the kingdom of God (John 3:3).

How are we born again? We act upon the divine influence which is God's grace upon our heart and the seed of God's word planted in our heart bursts forth and faith is born. We must confront the obstacles of lies and unbelief trying to hinder faith's birth and overcome it. There are many voices trying to get us to reject that influence. The devil does not want us changing our allegiance from him to God.

Just as a seed planted in the ground bursts forth and the young plant, tree, etc. becomes visible, saving faith that has burst forth in our heart is visible. We cannot have encountered Jesus Christ and it not become visible by our actions, our speech, and our life. I am not saying that we become like Jesus overnight. It takes time to become the new creation in Christ, the old things keep passing away daily as we read our Bibles, pray, live for Christ, and confront many obstacles (2 Corinthians 5:17). Nonetheless, the fact that we have encountered Jesus is seen at the inception of that encounter. We cannot go from dark to light and a change not be seen. If I turn on a light in a dark room, it's obvious that the light is there, no matter how dim the light may be.

Now, which scriptures planted in our heart that the divine influence or God's grace moves upon that causes us to act upon the word of God varies with the person. However, there are certain verses that influence all of us.

First, we must believe that God loves us and that His love sent Jesus to die on the cross.

> For God so loved the world, that he gave his only be-gotten son, that whosoever believeth in him should not perish, but have everlasting life (John 3:16).

Secondly, it is imperative that we believe that we are a sinner. We must believe that we have sinned.

> For all have sinned and come short of the glory of God (Romans 3:23).

Then if we believe that Christ died and rose again, we must confess it.

> That if thou shalt confess with thy mouth the Lord Jesus and shalt believe in thine heart that God hath raised him from the dead, thou shalt be saved. For with the heart man believeth unto righteousness; and with the mouth confession is made unto salvation (Romans 10:9–10).

What must be made clear here is that faith is needed but saving faith that results in salvation cannot be attained by man's efforts. Salvation is a gift of God through Christ's sacrificial death on the cross.

All our righteousness is as filthy rags (Isaiah 64:6).

Isaiah makes clear that our righteousness is nothing but filthy rags, and Romans 3:23 tells us that there is none righteous. Thus, any deed, work, labor, effort, etc. by us is as filthy rags. Filthy rags will not save us. There is not anything done by our effort that will save us.

This is sometimes difficult for us to accept or believe. You see we tend to think that we must have a part in our salvation. We want to be self-gratified. However, salvation is the gift of God, we can't work for the gift. Gifts are not worked for, they are given without payment on the recipients part.

God's gift is not earned, and it is not even deserved. If it was, then we would boast about all that we did. We would claim that because we did something that we deserved or earned our salvation.

Let's understand why any obstacle in this chapter is so vital to understand. The devil works overtime to stop us from becoming born again. Let me explain what this chapter teaches or reveals to us. It discloses that salvation is, in fact, a miracle. We are so set on sin, we are addicted to sin of all types. Before salvation, we are spiritually dead, and we need to be made spiritually alive. We dwell in darkness and must be translated into His Light (1 Peter 2:9).

Without faith in God's word, faith that believes God is, faith that believes that God loves us, faith that believes that God will forgive our sins, faith that believes that God will save us, faith that believes that Jesus died and rose from the dead because of our sins, any obstacle of lies or unbelief will stop salvation. If we do not overcome the obstacle, faith's birth will never take place.

What we must comprehend is the miracle that took place in our life when we acted upon His grace and influence upon our heart. In other words, our believing God's word planted in our heart, our act of faith enabled God to bring forth the miracle of salvation. We believed God, and we who were spiritually dead were made spiritually alive through the miracle of God. God transformed us from spiritual death to spiritual life.

This was made possible because we believed His word. We moved or acted upon His grace and He enabled us to believe. What happens is that God's word is planted, then God's grace or His divine influence moves upon our heart. When we act upon it and believe, faith is birthed and that enables God to perform the miracle of salvation. We don't save ourselves. It's God who performs the miraculous transformation from death to life in our spirits.

When faith birthed, we didn't think about it. We didn't ask if God really loves us? Will God really forgive our sins? Did Jesus really die on the cross and rise from the dead? Will God really save us? None of those questions were there. You see, God's influence upon our heart revealed to our understanding that He loves us, that we are sinners, that He will forgive us if we ask, that Jesus did die and rise again, and that He will save us.

When all those truths were believed, the miracle of salvation took place. According to Webster's dictionary a miracle is a supernatural event. A miracle is not a natural event. We must see the wonder that took place the moment we were saved. It was not anything that can be done in the natural. Anything that is supernatural is not natural, thus it is a miracle. Miracles are not natural; they are out of the ordinary and astounding.

When faith birthed forth, our faith enabled God to cause the spiritually dead to become spiritually alive. Salvation is an incredible miracle that causes us to see spiritually what could not be seen before. We were dead to spiritual truths and have been made alive to them. We believed, saving faith was born, and God performed the miracle of salvation. If we are saved, the faith of God has birthed in us.

Before faith can be what it should be in us, we must comprehend the incredible wonder, and the miracle of salvation that faith in God brought forth. We must comprehend that it was death to life and darkness to light. That same faith that birthed at salvation still resides in us. It is still alive in us.

In the forthcoming chapters, we will see many obstacles encountered on our faith journey. Only an understanding of faith's journey will enable us to overcome them. But first, we must understand that faith's birth is only the beginning of faith's journey. If God could cause us who were spiritually dead to become spiritually alive, why do we doubt that He can do whatever His word says? That's why the Lord wants us to comprehend the miracle that took place when we became born again.

Faith's Journey Confronts Obstacles: Instructing God's Soldiers to Overcome by Faith is meant to reveal that if we could believe that God could raise us from spiritual death to spiritual life, then He can do anything. God is not limited. It is us who limit Him through a lack of faith. The obstacles thrown at us by the enemy are to cause us to disbelieve God.

This book will reveal that the obstacles are needed for us to live victoriously on our faith journey. Obstacles or trials of our faith are part of faith's journey, and they strengthen our faith in God. These obstacles help God's soldiers to become proficient in His armor so that we can confront and overcome. Without the obstacles, we would never learn how the faith birthed in us at salvation can still enable God to do the miraculous in our life, if we only believe!

Chapter 2

Obstacle: Faith's Examination

But God led the people about, through the way of the
wilderness of the Red Sea: and the children of Israel went
up harnessed out of the land of Egypt (Exodus 13:18).

THIS CHAPTER WILL REVEAL a much-needed truth in our
faith walk and one that may not be known by many. I do believe
that some lack an understanding of storms, trials, or obstacles in
the Christian's life. Because of this lack, they are easily discouraged
when they are confronted by an unexpected obstacle.

We see in the verse in Exodus that God led the Israelites
through the wilderness. The Hebrew word for wilderness is also
a desert or a tract of land that is barren and unfruitful. This verse
refers to the deserts of Arabia which is a dry and unpleasant place.

I've titled this chapter as *Obstacle: Faith's Examination* which
is an obstacle of faith that must be understood. According to Webster's dictionary an examination is the act of examining; a careful
search or inquiry, with a view to discover truth or the real state of
things. Our faith is examined to see if it's genuine. Does our faith
have enough strength? Is it strong and founded on the truth of
God's Word? Or, is it weak and founded on falsehood? In other
words, what is the health of our faith?

Let's reveal this with more clarity. When we have a physical examination, what takes place? We're given various tests to see what condition our health is in. Well, after we're born again, I believe scripture reveals that our faith will have many examinations or tests to see if it is strong or weak, genuine or fake.

> And Jesus being full of the Holy Ghost returned from Jordan and was led by the Spirit into the wilderness. Being forty days tempted of the devil (Luke 4:1–2).

Exodus 32 tells us Moses was up on Mt. Sinai forty days. During the forty days without Moses, the Israelites turned aside quickly out of the way commanded by the Lord and built a golden calf to worship as their God. Then in Numbers 13–14, Moses sent out twelve spies into Canaan to search out the land for forty days. The number forty means probation or testing. Webster's says that probation is a trial or an examination. For this chapter it is an examination to expose the validity of our faith and the strength of our faith.

In chapter one, we saw what a miracle faith in God brought. We became born again, and we who were spiritually dead became spiritually alive. We walked in darkness and now walk in His Light. God delivered us with a mighty hand out of the bondage of sin and death.

Now, in the book of Exodus, there are all the plagues in Egypt and what God did to deliver the Israelites. There is no doubt that it was a mighty hand, especially the death of all the firstborn. Then Pharaoh pursues them to the Red Sea, and immediately the people complain. They accuse Moses of bringing them out of Egypt to die in the wilderness (Exodus 14:11–12).

Then in Exodus 14:21–22, God parts the Red Sea and it stood up as a wall on each side allowing the Israelites to cross on dry land. Yet, as they travel, they murmur and complain about everything. Often complaining that they were brought into the wilderness to be killed. They continuously disobeyed God. The manna was only to be gathered six days and yet they went out on the seventh. They built the golden calf. The epitome of disobedience is when they refused to go into Canaan because they believed the obstacle of the evil report. They missed God's Promised Land because of a lack of faith in the God who brought them out of Egypt with a mighty hand of deliverance.

Let's think about that. What are God's soldiers doing? Do we complain about the wilderness or the obstacle? Is it our job, our house, our car, our yard, our husband, our wife, our children, our finances, etc.? Do we complain because we want this, that, or whatever?

Our flesh is being discomforted and we don't like it. Thus, as God examines our faith's strength, He is finding it wanting. In other words, God is finding that we don't believe Him. We are looking at the obstacle and believing that it is greater than God.

Yet, when our faith birthed, we went from spiritual death to spiritual life. We believed God to perform the miracle and He did it. But now, in the wilderness, are we like Israel and wish we were back in Egypt, back in the world? Does the obstacle seem beyond God's ability? Are we like the Israelites and have forgotten our great deliverance at faith's birth? Have we forgotten the excitement when we became born again? We were on a mountain of joy. It was an incredible experience of being spiritually dead to being spiritually alive. We knew that God was real, and we were willing to die for Him. Of course, the Lord wants us to live for Him. The point here is that we were ready to do anything for the Lord.

Now, in the wilderness, have we become like the Israelites? Is denying our self or flesh too frustrating? Is the journey to the promise (seedtime to harvest) too long for our liking? Is the examination too tedious? Are we becoming weary? Do we constantly wish things were different? Do we wish for this or wish for that, or are we believing God and His word? Are we willing to confront until we overcome the obstacle and receive God's promise? Is God's word keeping our faith alive and strong? Are we believing His promises?

> And let us not be weary in well doing: for in due season
> we shall reap, if we faint not (Galatians 6:9).

And we know that all things work together for good to them that love God, to them who are the called according to his purpose (Romans 8:28).

If God be for us, who can be against us. (Romans 8:31).

But my God shall supply all your need according to his riches in glory by Christ Jesus (Philippians 4:19).

I have been young, and now am old: yet have I not seen the righteous forsaken, nor his seed begging bread (Psalms 37:25).

If we truly believe God and trust Him, then we are living in the will of God. Even the obstacle of the wilderness is His will. No matter how difficult on our flesh, He will make sure that we have the necessities of life that are food, clothing, etc. The Israelites were in the wilderness to have their faith examined, but they were given food, water, and their clothes never wore out. God supplied their need, but they lusted after their wants. During the examination, there must be self-denial to pass. If we have not learned the necessity of self-denial, we will never confront the obstacle and overcome it by faith.

Not that I speak in respect of want: for I have learned in whatsoever state I am, therewith to be content (Philippians 4:11).

What does content mean to us? I believe that it means to be satisfied in the will of God. We may not like it, but we are contented with the knowledge that God has brought us to this place to examine our faith. God has allowed the obstacle for us to once again believe in His ability to deliver us. We are confronted with obstacles so that we can learn to strengthen the faith that birthed in us at faith's birth. If we think about it, it was the size of a mustard seed. Yet, it enabled God to transform us from spiritual death to spiritual life. Now, He expects us to use our small faith until it becomes large (Mark 4:30–32). In other words, our faith was just a seed that germinated when it birthed, and now it must grow into a full-grown tree.

Let's look at a scripture that reveals why is it so vital that while we are in the wilderness, which is the time of the examination, to believe God?

> Because all those men which have seen my glory, and my miracles, which I did in Egypt and in the wilderness… Surely they shall not see the land which I sware unto their fathers…But my servant Caleb, because he had another spirit with him, and hath followed me fully, him will I bring into the land whereinto he went; and his seed shall possess it (Numbers 14:22–24).

Let's understand something here. This is the people that obeyed God to put the blood on the lintel and the two side posts for the death angel to pass over, witnessed the parting of the Red Sea, the manna, water from a rock, the pillar of fire by night, and the pillar of a cloud by day. But when told to go in and possess the Promise Land, they believed the evil report and not God. After all they had witnessed of God's ability, they did not have faith in God to perform His word.

What this reveals to us is that before we obtain the promise, there will be an evil report, which will be an incredible obstacle. Being aware of this truth can arm us with faith to believe God and not the evil report. We will receive God's promise, and we will receive an evil report. Will we confront the obstacle of the evil report and overcome it, or will we do as Israel?

Many times, I believe that the obstacle that we must confront will be an evil report. I remember when I was first born again, the enemy came at me with an incredible obstacle. He questioned if I was not born again before, what made me think that I was born again now? I was not learned in the Scriptures and was quite tossed about. I had no idea that if I was being attacked it was coming from the devil who is a liar (John 8:44).

When I went to my pastor at the time, I told him what was going on. He very calmly asked me if my life had changed. That was something that I knew. Before that night, I never read my Bible and only attended church on Christmas Eve. Now, I couldn't read my Bible enough, I was in church Wednesday night, and twice on Sundays. Plus, I attended a Friday night Bible study that a church member was teaching. Anyway, recognizing the truth of my changed life helped me confront the obstacle of lies and overcome. Only truth can overcome the evil report or the lying obstacle.

The question is will God's soldiers be like the Israelites, receive the evil report, and be overcome by its lies, or will we be like Joshua and Caleb, not receive the evil report, and overcome it with God's truth? Prayerfully this book will arm us with a greater knowledge of obstacles that will enable us to confront them and to overcome them by faith.

The other thing to remember about the Israelites exiting Egypt is that Exodus 12:37–38 states that six-hundred-thousand men on foot left Egypt. That number did not include wives, children, or the number of the mixed multitude. It had to be a few million. Even if we count only the men and their wives, that is one million two hundred thousand. Of the multitude twenty years and over, only Joshua and Caleb entered the Promise Land.

What is this revealing to God's soldiers? We see that during the examination an incredible number flunked, died in the wilderness, and never received the promise because of unbelief. Yet, they were excited when they were delivered from the Egyptian bondage. However, their faith was superficial, it had no roots as revealed in my previous book on storms. We see that during the checkup or examination, their faith was not strong enough to confront the obstacle of the evil report and believe that God would give them the Promise Land.

Luke chapter four reveals that Jesus was led by the Spirit (by God) into the wilderness and was tempted by Satan. Jesus was examined to see the validity of His faith in God. He was not only examined but went without food or drink for forty days.

What I want to interject here is that I believe that once we are born again, we are led into the wilderness where God examines the strength and the validity of our faith like what happened to me after my salvation experience. But I also believe that an obstacle or storm which is an examination follows any promise, word, or revelation from God. This was revealed in *Storms Are Faith's Workout*.

What we see in this chapter is that the multitude is delivered out of Egyptian bondage, a type of our deliverance from the bondage of sin and death. They overcame the obstacle of unbelief and God delivered them with a mighty hand. Then, they are immediately led by God into the wilderness to be examined. We see that most flunked and never received the Promise Land flowing with milk and honey.

Because of their unbelief, they had to wander in the wilderness forty years after Kadesh-Barnea, which was the entrance into the land of promise. Their wandering was one year for each day the spies went to spy out the land.

Let's think about that. We have been miraculously delivered out of the bondage of sin and death. When faith birthed in us, we were born again. We were resurrected from spiritual death to spiritual life. We are immediately led into the wilderness. I'm sure all of us remember the obstacles that we encountered when first saved. We questioned if we were really saved. We questioned if God truly loved us. We were overwhelmed by questions that didn't even enter our minds when we accepted Christ as Savior. If we had contemplated those questions, we would have been entertaining unbelief and would not have been saved. The devil tried to cast doubt about God's word to cause us to question our salvation. He did it to Eve in the garden where she questioned God's word. It worked so well then, that he uses it again and again to cause us to question God.

We must understand that if the devil can get God's soldiers to question what God has promised, we will not receive the promise. Only by using the faith that birthed in us when we were born again will we believe God. It is as we act on that saving faith that we will confront the obstacle of the evil report and believe God's report like we did at salvation.

It is being content without the leaks, onions, or wants during the examination that will enable us to trust God to remove the obstacle. Now, the length of the examination only God knows.

However, if we don't believe Him to help us confront the obstacle until we overcome, the examination can be lifelong as was revealed in my previous book about storms.

Let's understand what this chapter is about by asking some questions. First, why does God examine our faith? Second, why can't we get saved and go into the Promise Land? Third, why can't we receive a promise immediately without an examination? It is quite simple. It wouldn't take faith to go from Egypt to the Promise Land. It wouldn't take faith if we immediately received the promise. It is easy to live in plenty, but faith is the only way to overcome the obstacles that the enemy will put in our way. Even in the Promised Land, the Israelites had to confront and overcome the Canaanites. That's why we must learn how to confront and overcome by faith all obstacles in His armor.

Obstacle: Faith's Examination reveals the validity of our faith. Only the faith that birthed at salvation will overcome the obstacles, because it doesn't question God or His word. Faith that passes the examination doesn't believe any evil report instigated by the enemy, it confronts, overcomes the obstacle, and receives every promise that God has for His children!

Chapter 3

Obstacle: Faith's Armor

For he put on righteousness as a breastplate, and an helmet of salvation upon his head; and he put on the gar-
ments of vengeance for clothing, and was clad with zeal
as a cloke (Isaiah 59:17).

THE VERSE IN ISAIAH is referring to the awful day of God's
judgment. For this chapter, we are only concerned about the first
part of the verse that mentions two components of the armor of
God that Christians are to put on. It reveals how needed His armor
is, if God himself is clothed in it to go to war. How much more do
we need it?

Obstacle: Faith's Armor is to reveal another obstacle that
many Christians have a difficult time with. When faced with an
obstacle, we fight or do battle in our flesh instead of in the armor
of God. What happens when we use natural weapons? It's simple,
we compound the obstacle by using carnal means to do spiritual
warfare. The armor of God is not seen, so we forget about it and
do what comes natural in the flesh. Yet, Isaiah revealed that God
goes to battle in His armor. What is that saying to God's soldiers?

If we can start to visualize the armor of God in our mind's
eye, we will learn to confront the obstacle using it and not our

flesh. Ephesians 6:10–18 reveals God's armor. We will take a brief look at each of these verses to enlighten our understanding of the whole armor of God that is needed for us to confront and overcome by faith. Each piece of armor will become more enlightened as we progress in each chapter. This chapter is to begin our understanding of its use and start to instruct us how to overcome the obstacles that we face on faith's journey.

The armor of God becomes an obstacle because it is not the first outfit that God's soldiers go to war in. We are fleshly and revert to natural means when confronted with a battle. Christians must learn to utilize God's armor if an obstacle is to be overcome by faith. Instead, many are allowing the armor of God to become an obstacle and they are losing battles and not overcoming. Whenever we confront in the flesh, we will lose the battle. If we confront in the full armor of God, we will overcome. Putting on the armour of God should be as natural to God's soldiers as getting dressed in the morning. It's just something that we do automatically and that's what dressing in God's armor should be like.

> Finally, my brethren, be strong in the Lord, and in the
> power of his might (Ephesians 6:10).

This verse is a command to be strong in the Lord and in the power of His might. The Greek for *be strong* means to be empowered through the supreme in authority, to be increased in strength through God. *In the power of his might* in the Greek means in the ability of God's strength.

We are to be empowered through our union with Christ and draw our strength from the ability of God's strength. Our strength is not to be drawn from physical strength, but from God's supernatural strength that is unlimited. As a Christian, our strength does not come from our flesh, it comes from God. Christ is our strength. If we try to do spiritual warfare in our natural strength, we will fail.

> Put on the whole armour of God, that ye may be able to
> stand against the wiles of the devil (Ephesians 6:11).

The Greek to *put on* means to array with, clothe with, endue with. As we put on our clothes, we are to do the same with the full, the complete, or the total armor of God that we may *be able to stand against the wiles of the devil.* The Greek for *be able* means to be of power, and *to stand* in the Greek implies to be on its foundation, so as not to be overthrown or demolished.

What this is telling us is that to be able to stand means to be erect as a tree with its roots deep into the ground and the violent winds have no effect upon it. Therefore when the devil comes at us with his wiles, meaning his methods, his trickery which implies to lie in wait, we are not uprooted. In other words, the devil is a predator waiting to catch us off guard and attack. Satan waits for that weak moment, whatever it may be and attacks. That's why it is essential that God's soldiers learn the necessity of the whole armor of God, or we will try to fight the obstacle in the flesh. We cannot do battle in the flesh against a supernatural enemy.

A main point in verse eleven is that we are to *put on*. It is a command. *Put on the whole armour* is saying, "You put on the whole armour." That means that we are to clothe, dress, array ourselves with the total, the full, the complete, the whole armor of God. God has supplied the armor, but He will not dress us. The putting on or dressing ourselves is our responsibility. If we neglect the armor and are defeated, it is not God's fault. I will mention more about this in chapter four. God wants us to understand its necessity for our spiritual and physical life.

When my children were young, I would pick out what they were to wear. They were old enough to dress themselves, and I had everything ready. That is the way it is with the armor of God. He has everything ready for us, and we must put it on. It is only as we clothe ourselves with the whole armor that God has supplied will we be able to stand and be firm against the devil. The obstacles or his wiles will trip us up if we do not dress ourselves in God's armor.

> For we wrestle not against flesh and blood, but against principalities, against powers, against the rulers of the darkness of this world, against spiritual wickedness in high places (Ephesians 6:12).

We must understand that we do not fight against flesh and blood. We are not contending against human or physical opponents of the natural realm. Our opponent, the obstacle in our way, is not of this realm. We fight against principalities, against powers that are spiritual forces or influences. We fight against the rulers of the darkness of this world that have the qualities and attributes of Satan. We fight against spiritual wickedness meaning supernatural and demonic malice, plots, and strategies in high places which means the heavenlies or supernatural realm.

We do not fight or contend against physical or natural obstacles, they are supernatural. We fight the demonic spirits behind or controlling those who contend against us. Demonic plots or strategies are being planned in the supernatural realm and are carried out through those controlled by Satan in the natural realm. It looks like people, but it is not. The person or persons are being instigated by demonic forces that have control over them. All we have to do is see how hostile many people have become lately. That's why we must not react in our flesh or we will be helpless against the demonic power controlling the person or the mob.

Let me interject something here to help us to understand how the devil uses people. That means even Christians that do not use God's full armor. When I was first saved, an older woman in the church wanted to take me under her wings. I was young in the Lord and thought that would be helpful to me. She was very active in the church and I looked up to her. Anyway, she took me out for lunch one day. While we were eating, she told me that she was quite concerned for me. I was puzzled and asked her why. She told me that I was so heavenly minded that I was no earthly good to the Lord.

Eating my lunch was difficult after that. Everything in me was crying out to God and I just wanted to get home and pray. When I got home, I immediately went to my prayer corner in my bedroom. I cried out to the Lord to forgive me. If I was no earthly good to Him, there was no sense being here. I just wept and wept. Then when I calmed down, I heard the Lord speak to my heart. He said, "My Son was so heavenly minded and that is why He was so earthly good. If He had been earthly minded, He could not have performed His mission."

As I heard that, my heart was full of love for the Lord. At the same time, the Lord revealed that not all Christians are genuinely concerned for others. He revealed to me that she was jealous of my zeal. She had become so earthly minded that she had forgotten her first love. I must admit, that broke my heart as I had truly respected her. All I could do after that was pray for her, but I no longer trusted her counsel.

> Wherefore take unto you the whole armour of God, that
> ye may be able to withstand in the evil day, and having
> done all, to stand Ephesians 6:13).

The word *withstand* in the Greek means to stand against, to resist, or to oppose. *Having done all* means having worked out all things or everything. Again, we are told to take or put on the full armor that God supplies so that we can stand against, resist, oppose the devil's plots, malice, disease, etc. However, the key in this verse is *having done all*. It means that we have worked out everything. In other words, we know how to put the armor on and how to use it; we have proved it.

Remember in I Samuel 17 when Saul wanted David to use his armor, David refused because he had not proved it. David did not know how to use Saul's armor, so he used what he knew and had proven. He used God's armor. Of course, Goliath laughed at him, because he saw a young lad and not God's armor. The natural eye cannot see the armor of God, but the spiritual realm sees it. The devil knows if God's soldiers are clothed in God's armor or in our flesh. When he sees the armor of God, he knows he cannot overcome us unless he deceives us. He tries to make us believe an evil report and believe that we are no match, etc. In my book, *The Elfdins and the Gold Temple*, it shows how the devil through his follower deceived the Elfdins into thinking they had no power against him. They fell into four-hundred years of a dark age because of the enemy's deception. However, God tells us that if we put on His armor and stand, we will withstand, survive, resist, recognize, and overcome whatever the devil throws at us.

> Stand therefore, having your loins girt about with truth, and having on the breastplate of righteousness (Ephesians 6:14).

The Greek for *stand* means to be erect, upright, vertical. *Girt with truth* means to have no lies, no falsehoods. We are to stand in or with the truth of God and His word. *The breastplate* in the Greek means chest while implying lungs and heart which are needed for life.

Girt with the truth of God's word, we discover, we recognize, we see who our enemies are and how they come at us to attack. Through God's word, we recognize false doctrines, false beliefs, lies, deceptions, etc. With the recognition of these, we see where the enemy's snares are waiting to trip us up. That's why it is so important to know God's word. If we do not know the truth of what He says, we can be easily led astray by false doctrines.

Now, the heart is the seat of man's affections, loyalties, desires, etc. All our affections, loyalties, and desires stem or center in our heart. The breastplate of righteousness is, in fact, the life of God in the soul. Righteousness in our heart defines or determines everything on which our spiritual existence depends. The breastplate of righteousness defends the lungs and heart. This implies the heart's affections upon which spiritual life depends.

If our heart stops beating and we no longer breathe, we are dead. Using the breastplate to protect our heart and lungs implies that spiritual life depends upon righteousness being in our soul. Another way to explain it in simple terms is to ask ourselves who sits on the throne of our heart. Is it Christ or self? What this verse is revealing to us is that righteousness determines our spiritual life. Without righteousness there is no spiritual life. That's why the breastplate of righteousness protects our spiritual life from the attacks of the enemy.

> And your feet shod with the preparation of the gospel of peace (Ephesians 6:15).

The Greek for *feet shod* means to put on shoes or sandals. *With the preparation* means to be prepared, or ready to provide. The *gospel of peace* means that we are to bring the good message of the gospel that is a peace treaty between God and man. It is literally bringing peace, rest, prosperity, quietness in the lives of those who hear and receive it.

In Exodus 12:11, it is revealed that the Israelites were commanded to eat the Passover with their loins girded, shoes on their feet, and staff in their hand. They were to be prepared and to be ready for the journey. That is how it should be with us, we are to be ready at all times to provide the gospel of peace that will reconcile man to God. This can sometimes be an obstacle, for the enemy does not want us reconciling man to God. He will send every obstacle in his arsenal of evil to deter us. The whole armor must be put on, if we are to confront and overcome the obstacle.

> Above all, taking the shield of faith, wherewith ye shall
> be able to quench all the fiery darts of the wicked (Ephe-
> sians 6:16).

To make sure that no evil darts from the enemy penetrate our armor, we are to hold up the shield of faith. *Above all* means to lift up over or in front of our coverings or armor. Our shield of faith is held up to protect the body against the enemy's weapons. Let's understand something vital here. Satan's darts, his spears, his arrows, his missiles, etc. are inflamed with anger, grief, disease, lust, malice, etc. They are meant to destroy, not just to injure. He doesn't only want to destroy our faith, but to kill us.

As God's soldiers stand in faith, those fiery darts will be extinguished. Those darts are supernatural weapons and the natural man has no defense against them. If we try to fight in our flesh, we will end up like the sons of Sceva in Acts 19:13–16. Yes, they were not saved, but the point is they were in the flesh. The devil knows if we are dressed in God's armor or not.

> And take the helmet of salvation, and the sword of the
> Spirit, which is the word of God (Ephesians 6:17).

The *helmet of salvation* is our defense of the brain. It defends our brain against those thoughts or desires that could influence our thinking. Our thoughts are influenced by ourselves, family, friends, associates, news, the devil, etc. They are the voices constantly trying to sway what we believe or think. Only the *helmet of salvation* and the *sword of the Spirit which is the word of God* can help us to protect ourselves against the wrong thoughts.

The sword is of the Holy Spirit and He always acts in harmony with God's written word. God's word is quick and powerful and sharper than any two-edged sword (Acts 4:12). It is His living word that reveals the enemy's lies, tricks, snares, etc. When tempted, we need to quote the word which is the sword that will cut in pieces the snares of the enemy. God's word is life; the devil's lies are death.

> Praying always with all prayer and supplication in the
> Spirit, and watching thereunto with all perseverance and
> supplication for all saints (Ephesians 6:18).

The warfare that we are fighting against the devil is spiritual, and we need to see the importance of prayer and supplication. We are to be continuously petitioning God for ourselves and others. Perseverance means that we persist and endure with tenacity. We are ever watching for any attempt of the enemy to attack God's soldiers. When we perceive a scheme or maneuver, we immediately go into battle through prayer. Prayer is doing battle against the forces of Hell that would try to destroy, hinder, or weaken our resolve to continue. Through prayer, we work together with God to gain the victory and overcome Satan's obstacles.

Let's understand the importance of God's armor. Only it can equip us with all that is needed to stand against the enemy. We are engaged in a spiritual battle with evil. Satan will send obstacles that we will have to confront and overcome by faith our whole life. Please understand that our faith is examined continuously. We have to have physical exams our whole life to check our physical well-being and that is true with the examinations of our faith to check our spiritual well-being.

It is imperative that we do not go to war without our armor. We have daily battles with the devil, the world, and self. There are corrupt desires of the flesh that must be confronted. There are ungodly pleasures of the world trying to seduce us and they must be confronted. Evil is ever trying to grab hold of us in any form it can. Sin constantly lies at the door of our heart desiring us to yield. If we do what is well according to God, we will rule over the enemy (Genesis 4:6–7). As we stay dressed in God's armor, we will rule over sin.

God's soldiers must remember that we do not fight physical or natural opponents, but supernatural, evil, demonic spirits working through people in this realm. Hear me, it may seem like it is natural when looking at an individual, but it is a demonic spirit working evil through the person. Without the armor of God, we stand defenseless against the enemy. How can natural (flesh and blood) fight supernatural (spirit beings)? We cannot and that's why when we battle in our flesh we come away like the sons of Sceva. God's armor is meant to protect not only our spiritual life, but our natural (fleshly body) from supernatural opponents.

God's armor protects us defensively and offensively. It will protect us against any wile, trick, method, strategy, etc. that Satan may use. He has no wile that can overcome God's armor when we are fully armed in it. The armor protects us and the word of God (God's sword) will destroy and bring to naught the enemy's devices.

If we look at a knight fully armed before he battled, we will understand where we got the inspiration for the knight's armor from. Man took the armor of God and made his version of it. Of course, the natural armor was not infallible. However, God's armor is indestructible. Nothing the enemy does can destroy God's armor when we stand in faith. We cannot see the armor, but make no mistake, the enemy sees it.

Let me help us to understand how vital the armor of God is not only to our spiritual well-being but our physical well-being. If we do not put on the breastplate of righteousness, our heart and lungs are not protected. Spiritually, our heart is unprotected against wrong affections. Physically, our heart is not protected. How many get so angry and upset and have heart attacks? Without the helmet of salvation, our brain is unprotected. Spiritually against wrong thoughts and physically against tumors, etc. Without the girdle of truth, we are not protected against lies and false doctrines that are contrary to the truth of God or His word. Spiritually we are unprotected against lies. Physically, we are unprotected against lies that may claim that there is no cure. Through prayer, we stand in our armor and battle the enemy until the obstacle is eliminated.

Let me interject something here. When I was hospitalized for ulcerated colitis, I was told that I had to live with it. There was no cure. When the doctor told me that, I heard in my spirit, "That is a lie. I am He that healeth thee." Of course, I thought that I would be instantly healed, but I was not. When I sought the Lord, He told me, "Trust Me, I will lead you. Your body was created to heal itself. Follow My instructions, and I will heal you." Anyway, in the meantime, I was put on medication that had many side effects. When I was released from the hospital, I was on a strict diet that I stuck with, and I stayed on the prescriptions. At the same time, I began searching online for natural cures. It took time for me to get what worked for me, but I was able to quit the prescriptions. I have been eating normal, adhere to the natural supplements, and I am fine. That was seven years ago. If I had believed the evil report, I would not have confronted it in the armor of God, prayed it through, and would not have overcome. If we confront in our flesh without the armor, we will be defeated.

Once we daily dress ourselves in God's armor, we will be enabled to resist the tendency to battle in our flesh. This tendency is an obstacle that must be confronted and overcome by faith. We must quit looking in the natural realm of our flesh and rise above into the spiritual realm where the armor of God is. Understand that God's armor is vital if we are to continue faith's journey that began at faith's birth!

Chapter 4

Obstacle: Faith's Nemesis

> And it came to pass, when Pharaoh had let the people
> go, that God led them not through the way of the land
> of the Philistines, although that was near; for God said,
> Lest peradventure the people repent when they see war,
> and they return to Egypt: But God led the people about,
> through the way of the wilderness of the Red Sea: and
> the children of Israel went up harnessed out of the land
> of Egypt (Exodus 13:17–18).

CHAPTER THREE DISCUSSED THE armor of God, its components, its use, and the need for God's soldiers to be clothed in the full armor of God for spiritual survival. This chapter will again reiterate the need for God's armor and its function, while revealing that the examination is to help us to learn to first use the armor to confront faith's nemesis and overcome it. Many think that the enemy of their faith is the devil, when in actuality it is self or our flesh. Although chapter two used Exodus 13:18, this chapter will expound more on verse 18, while using verse 17.

Obstacle: Faith's Nemesis is to reveal that the obstacle of God's soldiers is going to war without the full armor of God and leaving their faith unprotected. In the previous chapter, it was made known that we tend to react to obstacles in our flesh or natural man. While this chapter is somewhat similar, we must understand that we are in the Army of the Lord and we are in a war to live by faith. How many times have we sang *Onward Christian Soldiers* since saved? How many times have we seen actual soldiers in battle? Have they been without their uniform? What we have to understand is that we are soldiers and we are expected to go to war in the uniform that our King has issued. We are fighting for the Kingdom of God and His righteousness against the kingdom of Satan and his unrighteousness. It is a war of faith verses a war of unbelief.

Now, God led the Israelites the long way around to the Promise Land. God knew that if the people were confronted with war, they would repent. They would be sorry or wish they had not left Egypt and flee back. It's quite clear that the repent is not a godly sorrow that leads to repentance (2 Corinthians 7:10). Let's understand something here, God led them the long way around because they would not have confronted the obstacle and overcome by faith. Instead, they would have fled back to Egypt. God was making it more difficult for them to return to Egypt. The long way around was for their good. They were heading to the Promised Land and God wanted them to get there.

The long way around was going to be difficult on their flesh, but it was needed for them to learn to confront it and overcome their flesh by faith. Sometimes, after we have been given a promise, it seems like we are going the long way around. But it is to force us to confront our flesh that is an enemy of our faith. Our old nature will never yield to God's will. Therefore, it will fight against the spirit continuously (Galatians 5:17). It is not good when God wants us going one way, and we go another way to avoid confronting our flesh. Our spiritual growth is contingent upon confronting and overcoming all obstacles by faith and that includes confronting and overcoming our flesh.

What must be understood is that God is always merciful. He was mindful that although they *went up harnessed,* meaning as fully armed soldiers, their years of slavery by the enemy had not taught them how to use God's armor. They were not ready to do warfare against an enemy. Let me explain what this means. When we are born again, we have access to God's full armor. But we cannot do battle with armed enemies until we learn how to use the armor. God's armor is only as capable as our faith. We must have faith in its proficiency, or it will be ineffective. God's soldiers need to understand that it is the armor of God that is faith's protection. The first place to use it is against our fleshly appetites that are founded in the lusts of the flesh, the lusts of the eyes, and the pride of life. These desires are the nemesis of faith in God. They are only concerned about satisfying their lusts or wants.

It is through the examination of our faith that we learn to confront our flesh and overcome it by faith. God's full armor is our defense and offense during the examination. If we don't have the examination, we will never learn to confront our flesh which is where we first learn how to use the armor.

Let's understand why it is imperative that God's soldiers become proficient, I mean masters in the use of God's armor.

> For though we walk in the flesh, we do not war after the flesh: For the weapons of our warfare are not carnal, but mighty through God to the pulling down of strongholds; Casting down imaginations, and every high thing that exalteth itself against the knowledge of God, and bringing into captivity every thought to the obedience of Christ (2 Corinthians 10:3–5).

If we cannot use the armor effectively to combat our own flesh, we will never be able to do spiritual warfare against evil forces of the devil and triumph over them. We must comprehend that we do not engage in warfare (military campaign with its arduous duties) in the flesh or our human nature with all its frailties and all its moral weaknesses. Our weapons are not carnal or that which is human, but mighty, powerful, and capable through God. The terms in these scriptures are military which means they are characteristic of soldiers. All Christians are soldiers of God Almighty and we are not to confront a supernatural enemy in the natural. Only God's weapons are capable of bringing down the enemy.

If we have not learned to use God's armor to confront our flesh, we will never be able to confront a supernatural enemy out to annihilate us. Our faith is unprotected without the armor of God. That's why faith's nemesis becomes an obstacle that gives place to the devil, because without faith in God's armor we will be defeated in our flesh. There is no faith to overcome a supernatural enemy in our natural or fleshly weapons, and we could be easily seduced into believing any evil report Satan hurls at us.

Some are probably wondering how can we use the armor against our flesh. It was revealed somewhat in chapter three, but let's look at a few components again to clarify its use. The breastplate of righteousness protects our heart against wrong affections. Our loins girt with the truth of God's word enables us to recognize wrong doctrines and to reveal where the enemy lies in wait to deceive us. The shield of faith prevents any fiery darts of the enemy penetrating our armor. The helmet of salvation protects our brain or mind against wrong thoughts or entertaining the devil's lies. The sword of the spirit is the word of God that will cut to pieces any snare of the enemy. Prayer is the spiritual weapon that aligns us with God and His will to strengthen us to stand.

As God's soldiers learn to use the armor to confront fleshly appetites, supernatural enemies will be easier to confront. It is our fleshly desires, fears, wants, etc. that are faith's nemesis and hinder us from confronting the obstacles. That's why we must be proficient in the use of God's armor and not use our own resources. Our flesh and blood armor or our human weapons are powerless against a supernatural enemy. It would be like putting up a hand to stop an atomic missile. Sounds a little ridiculous, but that's what many of God's soldiers are doing.

God's weapons cast down man's imaginations, man's reasoning, and man's knowledge. That's why it is imperative to realize that whatever we see, hear, or read influences our thinking. Our thinking is manipulated by whatever is fed into our brain. That's why we must have mastered the use of the helmet of salvation. We must not allow ourselves to be influenced, swayed, or persuaded to believe anything contrary to God's word or God's promises.

God's soldiers cannot allow faith's nemesis, meaning their flesh, to become an obstacle because they are not clothed in the full armor of God.

As I interjected in chapter three, if I had not used the helmet of salvation and had my loins girt with truth, I would have believed the evil report of the doctor. As I prayed and trusted God, the armor protected me, and I believed God. Yes, I had a long confrontation until I overcame. But that is what must be done. As stated in my book, *Storms Are Faith's Workout*, overcoming is based upon our love for God and believing in His love for us. Now, in this book, God's soldiers must confront, stand fully dressed in God's armor, until we overcome by faith. We must hold the line at all times and allow no breach of the enemy. It is us who have the overcoming weapons and we must not permit the devil to make us think otherwise. He is a liar and will do whatever he can to convince us to run instead of to stand by faith.

At this time, I will put in a little promotion for my fiction book done as an allegory. *The Elfdins and the Gold Temple* takes place in a supernatural world where evil did not exist until an evil prophet entered by deceitful means. He trained one of the Elfdins in the ways of black powers. This evil Elfdin convinced the others through deception that they had lost the supernatural powers given to them by the Sovereign God. Faith's nemesis, their flesh, became an obstacle, because they believed the lies.

That is what the devil tries to do to us. He works overtime to convince us that God's word is not true. Of course, that is what he did to Eve (Genesis 3:1). Once he influences us to doubt or question God's word, that is when we go from faith in God to unbelief. If we are to overcome the devil's lies, we must be clothed in God's armor.

If God's soldiers don't use the full armor of God, all that is seen, heard, or read will enter into the heart unfiltered. That means all that is impure or contrary to God will become part of our affections. However, if we use the full armor of God, we are enabled to take every thought, our thinking, our logic, our reasoning, and filter them to make them obedient to Christ. Faith's armor enables us to cast down or bring to naught all influences of our thinking that are against Christ.

Let me interject a vision that the Lord gave me many years ago concerning His armor. I was doing a week-long revival and before this particular night's meeting, I was praying about the lack of victory in Christians and the Lord showed me this. It was like the War of Independence. I watched as soldiers came back on stretchers, carts full of soldiers with legs missing, arms gone, heads wrapped, eye patches, and all were bloodied and messy. I asked the Lord what this was all about, and He took me to the place where they had started from before going to war. As I looked, I saw piles of shoes, helmets, breastplates, shields, girdles, and swords. God said to me, "My people insist upon going against the enemy without my full armor and they are wounded, discouraged, and even destroyed. I have supplied the armor, but they are not using it. Then, they accuse Me of not helping, not protecting, not loving, and forsaking them."

God makes clear that we are to put the armor on, He does not dress us. We are soldiers and we are capable of dressing ourselves. It's time for the soldiers of God to reassess how they go to battle. If we have not learned how to use the armor, we had better start today. Begin by understanding how each piece works and then see yourself putting it on. Continue to grow by studying the word to have the wherewith to answer him that reproacheth you (Psalms 119:42).

Okay, what is that all about. To explain, let's go back to the opening scripture in this chapter. We see in verse eighteen that the Israelites went up harnessed which means they had on armor, they were able bodied soldiers, and were armed. Because faith's armor was ignored, faith's nemesis or their flesh became an obstacle that they did not overcome. They listened to evil communications around them and continued to spread it from one to another. The more they listened and repeated what they heard, the more it influenced their thinking, and their heart or their affections lost faith in God.

The evil communications or evil reports influenced fear in their flesh and allowed their thinking and affections to sway from God, God's word, and God's will. We must understand that faith's soldiers main defense must be against all those influences that affect our thoughts or that which we meditate upon. Whatever influences our thinking is Satan's major stronghold. As the Israelites let evil reports influence their thinking, they constantly allowed their flesh to rule. They were overtaken by fear instead of faith in the God that had delivered them from Egypt. Thus, they didn't use God's armor and weapons that were capable of destroying the enemy's lies, deceits, influences. They did not confront their flesh with God's armor to protect their mind, therefore, they did not overcome by faith.

That's what is happening to God's soldiers today. God revealed in the vision that most are going to battle without the whole armor. It takes time to learn to be competent with its use. In today's world, all the instant this and instant that has caused many to be impatient in waiting. How many won't take time to learn something or to overcome an obstacle? But doing spiritual warfare without the armor of God will cause us to come back like the soldiers in my vision where faith's nemesis became an obstacle. God has given us all that we need to confront and overcome our flesh by faith, but we must use it. Like Joshua and Caleb, we must use the examinations in the wilderness to become proficient in the use of God's armor which will confront faith's nemesis and overcome it by faith!

Chapter 5

Obstacle: Faith's Love

And Jesus said unto him. Thou shalt love the Lord thy
God with all thy heart, and with all thy soul, and with all
thy mind (Matthew 22:37).

THE OBSTACLE IN THIS chapter that hinders God's soldiers
from loving God with our all is the love of self. Although it is similar to chapter four in that it deals with our flesh being the nemesis
of faith. It will reveal it in another way to clarify how our old nature
is forever the enemy of our faith in God.

We can never love God as His word says, until we confront
and overcome the love of self. According to Webster's dictionary,
love for God means an esteem and reverence with the fear of offending Him. That means that we will do anything so that we do
not offend, insult, misuse, or exploit His grace and His love that
has been freely bestowed upon us.

The verse in Matthew says that we are to love God with all
our heart. Let's again look at our heart. We touched on it in the
previous chapters, but I think that we must understand our heart
is the center of our feelings. It is the center of everything that we
care for. It is the focus of all our inward affections, all that we care
about, all that we love, or all that matters to us. If God is not all

that concerns His soldiers, we have an incredible obstacle to confront and overcome by faith if we are to continue faith's journey. We have not learned how to use God's armor to protect our heart from other affections.

Now, the second point in the verse is that we are to love God with all our soul. Our soul is our very breath. It is our very life. That means that we are to love God more than our own life. If you have not read my first book, *Storms Are Faith's Workout*, I go into some detail about self-love. I do believe that both books are needed to fully comprehend how to overcome. In this book, I am exposing obstacles that must be confronted and overcome by faith. However, this chapter's main focus is the obstacle of our flesh. As previously stated, if we can't confront our flesh and overcome it, we will never be able to overcome our supernatural enemy. If God's soldiers can learn to use His armor to confront and overcome our flesh by faith, we will live a victorious life in Christ.

The next point in Matthew 22:27 is to love the Lord our God with all our mind. The word mind in the Greek means our intellectual power, our understanding. It is the power that conceives, judges, or reasons; it is our remembrance.

Through the power of the mind that conceives, judges, or reasons, comes our intentions, our purposes, and our designs. What we hear, what we see, and what we read are all media that enter our mind. It is in our mind that we conceive, judge, and reason what has entered. How we reason it out determines our actions and our beliefs. All that we do is the result of what has entered into our thought process. Our mind is the center of our will, and our will is where we choose to believe or not to believe something.

Whether we believe God or man is our choice. We alone choose to do good or evil. The truth that man has been given the free will to choose good or evil is seen in that Adam had the choice to eat or not to eat of the tree of the knowledge of good and evil (Genesis 2:17). We choose to do God's will or our will. What we choose stems from whether or not we love God or self. Do we esteem and reverence Him with the fear of offending Him? The love means to have a high regard and hold in deep affection. This love is an incredible affection that chooses God above all else.

The fear this love has is not to be afraid or frightened. It is the desire to please and not to displease God. What happens here, is that the deep affection or deep regard that God's soldiers feel for Him and His divine character causes us to hate and shun anything that could offend such a holy being. All of what we do stems from our mind. That's why the helmet of salvation is so vital. If we don't control what goes into our mind, we will not be enabled to love God above all else.

What we must comprehend is the greatest need of defense in God's soldiers is our mind. It is our thoughts, what we think, and meditate upon that must be protected. When we dwell upon thoughts, we meditate upon them. This means that we keep allowing that thought to control our thinking. Are these thoughts God-centered or self-centered? Do they contain faith or unbelief? Are they godly or ungodly? Are they righteous or unrighteous? All thoughts that enter our mind must be equated with the truth of God and His word. That's why we must have our loins girt with truth to recognize the enemy's lies and know where he is lying in wait to trip us up.

As the mind is where we reason out our thoughts or the things that we choose, it is also where all our thoughts are stored. Our mind is our computer bank. Our memory is where we store all our thoughts. Now, as we read or hear God's word, we think upon His rules, His ordinances, His laws and then keep them in our memory. We keep them in our memory so as not to forget them.

> If any man come to me, and hate not his father, and mother, and wife, and children, and brethren, and sisters, yea, and his own life also, he cannot be my disciple (Luke 14:26).

The hate in this verse means to love less. It is telling us that we must love Jesus more. In other words, we must not love anyone, including self or our own life more than Jesus. We must love God so much that we are ready to give up or do anything to please Him. All other loves must be like a hate when compared to our love for God. This means that there must be no other affection that comes close to our love for God. That can be heart wrenching at times, as some of our loved ones will choose to forsake us because of our love and devotion to God.

Let me interject another example. My son had gotten on drugs and was deep into hard rock. I told him that it was not allowed in my house. He was forbidden to do any of it in our home. He went to the youth pastor of the church who rebuked me. The young pastor told me that I was going to lose my son if I didn't let him do what he wanted to do. He said that I cannot force my convictions on my son, that he must choose for himself. I told him that it was my house and my convictions are what is done in it. He proceeded to say that my son would hate me. At first I was dumbfounded, but I cried out to the Lord in my spirit. He told me that if I chose my son over Him that my son would be lost. However, if I chose Jesus over my son that he would be saved. I believed God and was quickened to Luke 14:26. It doesn't mean that I don't love my son, it means that I love God more. The devil wants us to choose any god other than God. If we love them more, they become our god. God will have no other gods before Him (Exodus 20:3).

When we love God with all our soul, we love God with all our life or with every breath. Only as that is a reality in our life will we be ready to give up our life for His sake, to endure whatever trials, and to be deprived of comforts rather that dishonor Him. God's soldiers dress in His armor, confront our flesh, and overcome it by faith to please God.

What we must understand is that to give up our life means that we give up the rights to our life or to live our life our way. To follow Jesus, we must give up what self wants. We must daily deny what we want (Luke 9:23).

Jesus is our existence. He is our life. Without Him, we can do nothing. Without Him, we are nothing. We have no life; our life is in Him (Acts 17:28). That's what deny self is all about. It is realizing that we only have life because of Jesus, and we gladly deny it to please Him.

To love God with all our heart, soul, and mind means to give over the rights to our life to Christ. We denounce all self-dependence and selfish pursuits. Our dependence is on God. We abandon our pursuits, our goals, our desires to follow Christ. His will for our life becomes our goal, our desire, etc.

None of us can follow Christ and continue on faith's journey unless we have learned to use God's armor to protect our mind. What we think will enter our heart and will consume our affections. We need the helmet of salvation to protect the mind and breastplate of righteousness to keep our affections towards God and Holy Spirit led.

Only self-love will prohibit God's soldiers from loving God with our whole being. We must understand that whatever we love most has our heart's affection, our thoughts, our life's pursuits, and our worship. We either love God or self. There are no other choices. Even if we love someone else more than God, it is still choosing self. It is what I want to do, what I want to have, what I want to worship, etc. If it's not love for God, it's love for self.

In order to put on God's armor, we must choose to love Him above all else. Only then will we be willing to protect our mind and our heart from wrong thoughts and wrong affections. *Obstacle: Faith's Love* can be a hindrance to faith's journey, if we do not confront self-love and overcome it by faith. Once we conquer the nemesis of our faith which is our old nature, our flesh, and self-love, then faith's love that must be God is not an obstacle. Faith's love or love for God will always be an obstacle as long as self-love rules in our heart. What that means is that as God's soldiers choose to deny self, we will be enabled to love the Lord our God with all our heart, and with all our soul, and with all our mind!

Chapter 6

Obstacle: Faith's Purge

I am the true vine, and my Father is the husbandman. Every branch in me that beareth not fruit he taketh away: and every branch that beareth fruit, he purgeth it, that it may bring forth more fruit. Now ye are clean through the word which I have spoken unto you. Abide in me, and I in you. As the branch cannot bear fruit of itself, except it abide in the vine; no more can ye except ye abide in me. I am the vine, ye are the branches: He that abideth in me, and I in him, the same bringeth forth much fruit: for without me ye can do nothing. If a man abide not in me, he is cast forth as a branch, and is withered; and men gather them, and cast them into the fire, and they are burned (John 15:1–6).

AS WITH THE PREVIOUS chapters, we will learn another obstacle. This one is again determined by our love for God or self. Purging is extremely painful at times. It is never comfortable on our flesh. If we have not chosen to deny self, we will not be purged to bring forth more fruit. Everything centers upon our free will. God will not make us serve Him, and He will not force us to go through any pruning. If we are not willing to let something go for

His glory, we will wither until we are not bearing any fruit. In other words, we will become a barren or fruitless tree.

Without pruning, there is no purifying, no separating, no cleansing of whatever is impure. Common sense reveals that if we don't prune in the natural, the trees become a tangled mess and full of sucker branches choking fruit. In the spiritual, it means that we become more entangled with the things of this world and full of unbelief. We refuse to separate ourselves from what is impure and cleave unto what is defiling, destroying, or choking any fruit that we may have been bearing.

Jesus says that if pruned, God's soldiers will bring forth more fruit. What that means is not only in quantity, but in quality. Our fruit will multiply in number and be richer and more exceptional fruit. What helps cleanse us is His word. The word will clean or make free from dirt or impurities. We are sanctified and cleansed with the washing of water by the word (Ephesians 5:26).

The Husbandman is God the Father. All pruning is done by Him. The reason that He prunes us is to remove whatever is not pure. That means all that is mixed with something else. Our faith is not unalloyed but alloyed. It is mixed with other beliefs, logic, etc. All impurities must be removed if we are going to bear pure fruit. We cannot bear more fruit in unbelief, we must possess unalloyed faith.

Although education is good and beneficial, we must be careful that we don't rely on man's ability, man's wisdom, and man's knowledge. What this means is that God's soldiers must not base faith on man's knowledge, beliefs, teachings, science, medicine, etc. Anything other than faith in God, His ability, His wisdom, His knowledge, His word, etc. is impure. All that is not faith in God must be purged or it will hinder our fruit bearing.

What we must understand is that it is not only our love for anything or anyone more than God that must be pruned, but our belief in whatever is of man. Sometimes our education can hinder our belief system, for we tend to rely more on what we have been taught by man than on what God wants to teach us. Faith is like stepping out on the water and walking across to dry land.

We would rather row the boat into the land. That is the difference between faith and unbelief. It is the difference between trusting our ability and trusting God's ability.

> But without faith, it is impossible to please him: for he that cometh to God must believe that he is, and that he is a rewarder of them that diligently seek him (Hebrews 11:6).

Only faith pleases God. This faith in the Greek means to have firm persuasion, full confidence, or trust in God. True faith or pure faith is freedom from all doubt. Faith that doubts is not pure faith. To doubt is to question, to fear, to distrust, to hesitate, etc. It is to have uncertainty of mind. Doubt causes our mind to fluctuate, to waver, to stagger respecting truth because of a defect in knowledge. This was revealed at length in my first book, *Storms Are Faith's Workout* in chapter five. Any defect in our knowledge can cause us to have a misinterpretation of God.

If we lack knowledge about someone or we don't truly know them, we can't truly trust them. It is quite difficult to put our trust in someone that we don't know. That's why we must know God's word. The more of God's word we hear, the more knowledge we receive about Him (Romans 10:17). The more of God's word in us, the more we can know about God. The more we know about God, the more we are enabled to trust Him. When we truly understand that He is the God who spoke all things into existence, the God who parted the Jordan, the God who rose Jesus from the dead, the God who can do the impossible, we trust Him with our life.

We can never have too much of God's word, because we can never have too much knowledge of God. As a matter of fact, the more we know Him, the stronger our faith in Him becomes. Stronger faith means the easier it becomes to trust Him when the pruning starts.

Trust is the key to allowing Him to prune us. We may think that we need something, but God says it must be pruned. Although we may not enjoy it, we trust Him to bring us through it bearing more fruit. Because we desire to please Him, we confront the pruning and overcome it by faith. Just as a tree might not like us cutting off certain branches, we may not enjoy the pruning. However, without the pruning, we will never bring forth the fruit of the Spirit needed to overcome this life.

Let me interject an example of pruning in my life. As a young Christian, I had read Ephesians 5:19 that we are to speak in psalms, hymns, and spiritual songs. When I read it, I sat back and knew the Lord was speaking to me. At the time, I must have had thousands of songs and they weren't spiritual. I could feel the turmoil in me and asked the Lord what I was supposed to do with all my songs? I must add, that I did not drink, do drugs, or smoke, but I was addicted to the music. It was like asking me to cut off my arm or leg. As I continued to pray, the Lord reminded me of the sermon that I heard that Sunday that we need to be transformed by the renewing of our minds (Romans 12:2).

It was a challenge, but I knew that the Lord was making clear that if I wanted to grow in Him that my mind must be renewed. He made clear that the worldly music must go, or it would hinder me from being what He wanted for my life. There was no doubt about it, I needed to be pruned. It was painful on my flesh, but I discarded all the music. Of course, I see the fruit of it now and that if I hadn't submitted to the pruning, I would not have been enabled to do what He has called me to do. It would have kept me with one foot in the world and the other foot in Christianity. In other words, I would be a lukewarm Christian bearing no fruit for the Lord.

We must be careful not to listen to the voices that cry out to us so loudly that we can't let that go. Or it's not that bad. How is what I'm doing hurting anyone? It's my life and God wants me to be happy. Reality is that we are hurting someone and that is our own soul. God doesn't want our flesh satisfied and our soul withering. That's why Jesus said that if we are to follow Him, we must deny self (Matthew 16:24).

The devil sends his darts, logic cries for us to believe it, science claims that it has evidence, medicine says that this is how it is taken care of, psychology says that it's not your fault, false teachers teach what is contrary to sound doctrine, and self-yields to the lusts of the flesh, the lusts of the eyes, and the pride of life. All these voices clamor to be heard over the still small voice of the Holy Spirit that is trying to prepare God's soldiers to be Christ's bride.

If we have learned to dress daily in the armor of God, we will have acquired the ability to recognize all these impure voices that want us to wither until we are fruitless. What happens when we ignore the armor is that our mind hears all the contrary voices which we then think on. All contrary voices are lies, because anything contrary to God's truth is a lie.

What happens is that we do not confront the voices and overcome them by faith. Instead our mind thinks on or meditates on all these so-called rational, logical thoughts, what we are seeing in the natural, and we waver. We become so full of worldly knowledge that it causes us to doubt God's word.

In this chapter, we must see the importance of being pruned from all that is contrary to faith in God. We understand that God is the Husbandman that purges. He takes away all that is impure and the only thing that is pure is fruit as a result of genuine faith in God.

But how does God purge us of all that hinders our fruit? Does He just say, "Be gone self, logic, science, medicine, false teaching, unbelief, worldly music, drugs, alcohol, cigarettes, etc.?" Of course not, He can't make us think or do anything that we don't want to. We have a free will to think or to do whatever we want.

Let's look at a scripture that helps us to understand how the pruning takes place. God helps us turn from wrong thinking by trying us. In other words, He turns up the heat.

> Wherein ye greatly rejoice, though now for a season, if
> need be, ye are in heaviness through manifold temptations: that the trial of your faith, being much more precious than of gold that perisheth, though it be tried with
> fire, might be found unto praise and honor and glory at
> the appearing of Jesus Christ (1 Peter 1:6–7).

Trials, storms, or obstacles in our life are how God purges out all that is mixed in with our faith. As God removes all those impurities, all that is left is faith and faith in God alone. However, if we do not abide in Him, meaning to dwell in, to continue in, or to endure, we will not come through the pruning. In other words, we will not confront the obstacle of our flesh and overcome it by faith. Unless, God's soldiers are purged, there will be no fruit that pleases God. Instead of producing the fruit of the Spirit, we will produce the works of the flesh (Galatians 5:19–24).

As we endure each trial, storm, or obstacle, we come out with a stronger conviction of the truthfulness of God and the truth of His word. But if we listen to contrary voices and not the voice of God when the obstacle appears, we will worry, fear, doubt, not let something go, etc. We will be fruitless and nothing more than an unproductive branch drawing life from the vine but giving nothing back.

As I said earlier, education and knowledge are beneficial. However, we must not lean on them during the confrontation of obstacles. Only leaning on God, having total faith, complete trust in God is how these impurities are filtered from our thinking, our affections, our life. We must understand that the more we are tried (faith to faith) is how God purges or prunes all that is useless to renewing our mind and our faith in Him.

Our fruit must be pure. All hate, loathing, despising, jealousy, envy, prejudice, etc. must be purged to bring forth love. All distress, frustration, discord, disharmony, etc. must be purged to bring forth peace. All greed, indulgence, gluttony, debauchery, etc. must be purged to bring forth temperance or self-control. All impatience, rebellion, complaining, quick-tempered, etc. must be purged to bring forth long-suffering. Without purging that which hinders good fruit, we will not bear quality fruit.

Confronting obstacles is not pleasant, but without the process of purging, our faith is not purified. Just as gold is refined under extreme heat to purify it, our faith is put through a fiery furnace. The hotter the temperature, the more the impurities are forced to the surface and then purged.

Let me give an example of accepting or refusing the purging. If during the heat, the confrontation of the obstacle, we lean unto our own understanding or listen to contrary voices, the purging does not take place. What this means is that if we allow our flesh to convince us that the person does not deserve to be forgiven, the unforgiveness will not be purged. Now, if we lean on God and listen to His voice, our faith is purified. What this means is that if we listen to the Holy Spirit that tells us that we are only forgiven as we forgive others, the unforgiveness is purged.

That's why as God's soldiers, we must learn to be proficient in God's armor and use the shield of faith to prohibit contrary voices from getting near us. Along with the helmet of salvation, we can keep our mind free of whatever is not of God. As we keep our mind clear of contrary voices, the breastplate of righteousness will protect our heart from allowing affections that could hinder our loving God with our very being. Like I revealed earlier, if I wasn't willing to let go of the worldly music that the Lord wanted me to, I would not have been pruned. It is imperative that whatever the Lord wants us to let go of, we must freely allow Him to prune it out of our life. If we are pruned, we will bring forth fruit pleasing to God.

Faith's purge can become an obstacle any time we fight the pruning process with our flesh. This happens because we are not willing to put up with the pain or discomfort in our flesh. However, as we trust God and allow His voice to enter into our thoughts, we confront any contrary voices, overcome them by faith, yield to the pruning, and bear much fruit!

Chapter 7

Obstacle: Faith's Mind

And be not conformed to this world; but be ye transformed by the renewing of your mind, that ye may prove what is that good, and acceptable and perfect will of God (Romans 12:2).

FAITH'S MIND CAN BE an incredible obstacle to God's soldiers who are more inclined to use logic or reason than to think with the mind of faith. If we rely on man's knowledge, man's wisdom, man's education, we will not overcome the obstacle that wants us to do things our way.

The above scripture in the book of Romans tells us that we are not to be conformed to this world. If we are conformed to this world, we are fashioning self according to the manners, opinions, moral qualities, etc. of this present age with its course or direction that is in opposition to God's will. We are to be transformed which means to be metamorphosed, changed, transfigured in form or nature.

We are transformed by the renewing of our mind which means renovation. To renovate something is to make it new after decay, destruction, or depravation. If something is depraved it is in a condition where good qualities are lost. An example of good qualities being lost is to look at a rotten potato. Whew! Talk about a stinking savor. That is definitely what being depraved is like.

The reason faith's mind cannot be fashioned or conformed after this world must be understood. God's soldiers are not to go in the direction that is opposed to the Spirit of Christianity. In other words, the world's manners, opinion, and moral qualities are contrary to Christ. Everything about the world is the opposite of Jesus, for it is ruled by Satan who has blinded their minds (2 Corinthians 4:4). As the rotten potato, a mind controlled by Satan has no good in it. The more influenced by the devil the more evil are the deeds of the person.

Before we were born again, we lived according to this world. We lived in sin. We partook of pride, vanity, deceit, lies, fornication, adultery, pornography, drugs, etc. The course of the world was our direction, our way, our mentality, etc. In other words, we thought like the world, we acted like the world, we talked like the world with all their vulgar language, etc. We were worldly minded and worldly directed.

But now in Christ, our minds must be transformed or metamorphosed. This is not a simple change, but a total renovation. It is a severe and drastic change of our nature. When anything is metamorphosed, it is changed into something totally or completely different. For instance, a tadpole is changed or metamorphosed into a frog. A caterpillar is changed into a butterfly. The sinner is changed from spiritual death to spiritual life. These are drastic changes.

When something is renovated, it is made new after decay, destruction, or depravation. If we picture a house before it is renovated, we understand the change that takes place. Well, our depraved mind, our old nature, must be metamorphosed by a severe renovation. This must take place in our mind which is the center of our thoughts and our will. If the change or metamorphosis doesn't take place in our mind, there is no change in our life, our thinking, our direction, etc. Remember, all our choices come from what we think or meditate upon.

That's why if God's soldiers do not learn to use the helmet of salvation, our mind will keep being fed the ways, the mentality, the morals, etc. of the world. Because of our free will, we have the liberty to choose. In other words, we have the freedom of choice. We choose whether we yield our members as instruments of righteousness or as instruments of unrighteousness (Romans 6:13).

> Let this mind be in you which was also in Christ Jesus (Philippians 2:5).

The key word is *let*. Webster's says that it means to allow, don't prevent or forbid, allow to enter, or grant use of. In order for our minds to be transformed or metamorphosed, God's soldiers must allow or grant Christ the use of our mind. We must allow the thinking like Christ in our mind. This means that we freely give up our way of thinking and allow God's word to lead our thoughts, our feelings, and our will.

> He must increase but I must decrease (John 3:30).

How can the mind of Christ, which are His thoughts increase in us? And how can our mind, which are our thoughts decrease in us?

> And he said to them all, If any man will come after me, let him deny himself, and take up his cross daily, and follow me (Luke 9:23).

The key word in the above scripture is *deny* which means to deny utterly, to disown, or abstain. That means that to deny self means to disown or abstain from self. If we are to follow Christ, we must acknowledge that self doesn't belong to us.

> For ye are bought with a price; therefore glorify God in your body, and in your spirit which are God's (1 Corinthians 6:20).

We are bought with a price and have no rights to self. If we are Christ's, self belongs to Him. He is the one who paid the price. We must of our own free-will abstain from the use of our passions, our appetites, our wants, etc. If we don't do this, Christ cannot increase, and we will not decrease. Only as we choose to restrain from the use of self, will His mind or faith's mind increase in us until we are thinking like Jesus.

Jesus did always whatever pleased the Father (John 8:29). That is saying that everything Jesus did was agreeable, conformable, of one mind with God the Father. Jesus agreed with the Father; He walked in harmony with God (Amos 3:3).

Whatever Jesus did, the Father was with Him. They walked together because they were of the same mind. Jesus and the Father thought, felt, and willed the same. There was no controversy between them. They had no dispute, debate, or contrary opinions, because they were of one mind, one purpose, one desire, and one will.

How does faith's mind or Christ's mind always please God? It is quite simple. Faith's mind does all that is opposite of the world's mind because it has disowned or utterly denied self any place in its thoughts. It uses the helmet of salvation to keep its thoughts pleasing to God.

God's soldiers have learned to dress daily in the full armor of God. As we keep the helmet of salvation protecting our mind from wrong thoughts, wrong doctrines, etc., we are transformed daily by the renewing of our mind. Because we deny self, our thought pattern is renewed. Then, we are enabled to discern and to know the will of God.

That is what Jesus did and He was led by the Holy Spirit and not self. We cannot please or agree with God, if and when self leads or rules. God's soldiers must understand that self is fashioned after this world, its thoughts, its ways, its opinions, etc. All the world's ways, thoughts, etc. are contrary to God's. In other words, they are going in the opposite direction.

> For my thoughts are not your thoughts, neither are your
> ways my ways, saith the Lord (Isaiah 55:8).

Self is not capable of thinking like God because it is self-centered and not God centered. Because all the ways of self are in opposition to God, we must deny self in order to follow Him. Jesus understood the need to deny self. If He had yielded to His flesh or human nature, He would not have gone to the cross (Matthew 26:39). His flesh battled his Spirit, for they are contrary one to the other (Romans 5:17).

> And he came out, and went, as he was wont, to the mount of Olives: and his disciples also followed him. And when he was at the place, he said unto them, Pray that ye enter not into temptation. And he was withdrawn from them about a stone's cast, and kneeled down, and prayed, Saying, Father, if thou be willing, remove this cup from me: nevertheless not my will, but thine, be done. And there appeared an angel unto him from heaven, strengthening him. And being in an agony he prayed more earnestly: and his sweat was as it were great drops of blood falling down to the ground (Luke 22:39–44).

Jesus was in agony means that He was in torture of spirit. This torture caused Him such torment that He sweat blood. None of us have experienced such agony that our sweat ran down as blood. The struggle with our flesh is not a noble one like Jesus had in Gethsemane. We fight God because we want to hang onto something that He wants purged for our own good. We fight against the Lord because we don't like His will for our life at the time. We fight Him because we want it to be this way and God's will is the opposite. We fight because we don't understand that we are to trust His love.

Jesus didn't allow His flesh or self to rule. He denied its cowardice, its desire, and cried that God's will and not His be done. He abstained from thoughts of self and freely agreed to do God's will. He was led by the truth of God's word by remaining in prayer with His Father. Prayer gave Him the strength that He needed to fight His flesh. If Jesus had to pray, how much more do God's soldiers need to pray for strength to confront the obstacle of our flesh and overcome?

It wasn't dying on the cross that He struggled with, but Jesus had to suffer separation from God for us. When Jesus became sin for us, God the Father could not look upon Him. Their relationship was disconnected for the first time since eternity for us. We cannot imagine the anguish of soul that Jesus experienced because of us. It was my sins and your sins that caused His suffering. But He willingly obeyed God and ignored His cost to save us.

As God's soldiers, we must understand that is what faith's mind is all about. It is to abstain, utterly deny self what it wants, what it thinks, what it desires, what it wills, etc. Faith's mind has disowned self and self has no rights, no privileges, no claims, no birthrights, etc.

If we think that Jesus's human nature or self wanted to suffer such anguish, we are deceived. Self is not capable of anything that could please or be agreeable to God. But how can God's soldiers deny or abstain from self? We must have a radical change inward and outward. We must be metamorphosed. Our old nature must be transformed into the new nature created after Christ. That means that we allow our mind, the inner man, our inward being to be transformed through the knowledge of God's word. Then the inward change produces the outward change. A mere outward change is of little worth if the inward is still depraved, decayed, and filthy, meaning our thoughts, our ways, and our will are according to the flesh, self, or human nature. Such change is nothing more than a white-walled sepulcher full of dead man's bones (Matthew 23:27).

Faith's mind has been metamorphosed from self to selfless. It has been transformed from the old nature fashioned after the world to the new nature fashioned after Christ. This means that faith's mind is something totally different. It is a new creature and is nothing like it was. Just as the butterfly is nothing like the caterpillar. The caterpillar represents self and is earth bound. The butterfly represents the Spirit and is heavenly bound (2 Corinthians 5:17).

In order to not allow faith's mind to become an obstacle, we must allow the mind or thinking of Christ to permeate our very being. That is the only way that we will be enabled to discern what is the good and perfect will of God. This means that because faith's mind denies self and does not follow the morals, the ways, the thinking of the world, God's soldiers discern, know, follow whatever pleases or is agreeable to God because we are of one mind with Him!

Chapter 8

Obstacle: Faith's Foundation

In the beginning God created the heaven and the earth (Genesis 1:1).

Now faith is the substance of things hoped for, the evidence of things not seen. Through faith, we understand that the worlds were framed by the word of God, so that things which are seen were not made of things which do appear (Hebrews 11:1,3).

IN THIS CHAPTER, WE will learn that God's faith can be an obstacle to our faith. If we as God's soldiers do not understand the faith of God, we will be hindered in our faith journey. Only as we comprehend the foundation of faith can we confront obstacles and overcome them by faith.

Genesis makes clear that God created all things which means that God brought them into being. In other words, God caused to exist what previously to that moment, did not exist. In Hebrews 11:3, we understand that the things that are seen were not made of things which do appear. God brought into being by His faith, through His word, that which did not exist before He called it forth.

The previous chapters have been teaching different obstacles that must be confronted and overcome by faith. This chapter is meant to help us understand why there seems to be such a struggle in us concerning our faith.

Before God's soldiers can have overcoming faith, we must understand where faith originated. To comprehend that, we must first recognize that there are two worlds. There is the supernatural, spiritual, invisible world, and the natural, physical, visible world. Faith will not work unless we separate the natural world from the spiritual world. Please pay attention here and receive the revelation needed to revolutionize your faith.

Hebrews 11:3 tells us that the worlds were framed by the word of God. Faith is a superseding force in that it existed before the natural world existed. This informs us that faith was here before the natural world was created. That means that faith is part of the spiritual world or the world where God resides. In other words, faith is not part of this world which is natural and physical. Faith must be viewed as a supernatural entity.

We try to make faith part of the physical realm, when it is part of the spiritual realm. In other words, faith is not part of man's knowledge, man's logic, man's wisdom, man's science, man's medicine, or man's ability. Faith is not a physical component, it is a spiritual component. We must understand that faith began in eternity past in God which reveals to us that faith is part of God. It is an attribute of God; it is a characteristic quality of God. Since God is a spiritual, eternal Being, faith is an eternal force of the spiritual realm.

Now, faith's creator is God. Faith began in Him. That means that God who is perfect has perfect faith. There are no flaws in God's faith. The revelation of God's faith will transform our faith. That means it will fundamentally change the way we think. Until we comprehend the faith of God, we will continue to struggle with our faith.

Let's look at what we think of created as meaning in our natural man. We think of the potter molding clay to make something. We think of the fashion designer creating the latest fashions. We think of the artist creating his masterpiece. Yet, Hebrews 11:3 tells us that it was the word of God that framed, constructed, created the worlds. And the things created in the physical world were made of things that were not seen.

That is telling us that there was nothing visible here. The potter uses clay. The designer uses cloth, etc. The artists creates through the use of paints and a canvas. All create through materials that exist in the physical. God didn't have anything visible, physical, concrete, etc. God took faith and created the world. In other words, God used only His faith to create all that we now see in the physical world.

Faith existed before this world did, because God's faith created the universe, the sun, the moon, the stars, etc.

> I have declared the former things from the beginning;
> and they went out of my mouth; and I shewed them: I
> did them suddenly, and they came to pass (Isaiah 48:3).

Hebrews 11:1 says that faith is the substance of things hoped for, the evidence of things not seen. That means that faith is that which becomes a foundation for another thing to stand on. It takes faith to get substance. As God's soldiers, we must grasp hold of this truth to confront all obstacles and overcome them by faith.

God's faith was the foundation on which He brought forth the Heaven and the earth. God's faith was the foundation on which He created the world. His faith was the substance that enabled Him to speak forth and create. God believed and brought forth. We must understand that when His words went forth from His mouth, something that never existed was created from nothing. The substance was God's faith and it came forth in the snap of a finger, or as the Lord says in Isaiah that He did them suddenly and they came to pass.

How can God do such things? Because He has no unbelief, no doubt, no alloyed faith in His ability. To doubt or to have unbelief would be against His character. Why would it be against who He is? Because faith is one of His attributes. As God is holy, God is love, God is merciful, God is faith, etc.

If we are to understand why God has no unbelief, even knowing that He is faith, we must look at some of His other attributes that help us comprehend His faith.

1. God is Omnipresent. That means that God is present everywhere at all times seeing all that we do (Psalms 139: 7–8; Job 34:21).

2. God is Omniscient. That means that God is all-knowing. God knows our thoughts, what we will say, and what we need before we think or speak (Psalms 139:1–4; Matthew 6:8). There is nothing that God doesn't know. Even before He created man, He knew that he was going to fall. God already had the plan of salvation or Christ's death prepared (Genesis 3:15). Nothing takes God by surprise.

3. God is Immutable. This means that God is unchangeable. He will never change. What He was yesterday, He is today, and will be tomorrow (Malachi 3:6; Hebrews 13:8; James 1:17). All creation may change, but God will never change. If God changed, He would cease to be God. This is an important truth that must be understood. God cannot change, so His attributes are who He will always be.

4. God is Omnipotent. This means God is all-powerful. He possesses unlimited power which means that there is no limit to His power (Revelation 19:6b; Jeremiah 32:17). We must see the importance of this attribute to understand God and His ability. God can do anything, there is nothing impossible with God (Luke 1:37). This tells us that God is capable of doing what may seem impossible to us. There is nothing beyond the scope of His power.

Let's get back to the fact that God is a Spirit Being. He is eternal. When Genesis 1:1 says that in the beginning God created. It doesn't mean the beginning of God. God is eternal. Eternity goes forever in both directions, so to speak. He has no beginning or end. The beginning refers to this age or to time. Time started when God created the worlds.

Now, faith was and is part of the spiritual realm, it was here before creation. Faith is part of eternity. We must realize that faith will not work unless we separate the natural realm from the spiritual realm. Faith is not part of the natural realm of man's logic, man's understanding, man's science, man's wisdom, man's medicine, etc.

We try to make faith part of the natural realm when it is part of the spiritual realm. Faith's foundation is not based on our faith, our ability, or our power. Faith's foundation is based on God's faith, God's ability, and God's power. It is not faith in our faith, but it's faith in God, His word, His ability, and His power. It is God who brings forth what we believe Him to do. That's what faith is all about. Faith believes that God is able to do what He promises. Our faith is not in us or our ability. Our faith is in God and His ability.

I want to interject something that happened when my husband and I had taken on the remodeling of an old home in Connecticut for someone. Of course, it was mostly my husband. However, I had to make do without a kitchen for some time. The point that I want to bring out is that carpenter ants had eaten away the timber sill on a stone foundation under the kitchen. I'm talking about a beam eight inches by eight inches and about ten feet long. My husband had completely removed the old beam and was in the basement using jacks to lift the house to move the new beam into place. Mind you the house was three stories high. However, when he tried to force the beam into place, it would not go. He was on a schedule to get the house finished by such a time.

He tried for two days and was beside himself what to do. I sensed that the Lord wanted me to go upstairs and stand over the place where the beam needed to go in under the kitchen. I sensed the Lord tell me that I had on His armor and to pray. I stood there and told the Lord that I believed He could do anything. Then I said, "Father, only you can perform the miracle that is needed here. You are our God, and nothing is impossible with you." I then stretched forth my hands over the spot and said. "In the Name of Jesus, show my husband the power of the God that he serves."

The next thing that I knew, I and the house was lifted up, and I heard this load noise. I got my bearings and immediately ran down to the basement and found my husband and my oldest daughter (Dawn) standing away from the spot, their mouths were wide open, and their eyes bulged. My husband couldn't speak, but my daughter said, "Mom, the house lifted up and the beam went into place all by itself. Dad was trying to put it in and fell forward as the beam jumped into place all by itself." I looked at my husband, and he shook his head and said, "Just before the beam jumped into place, the Lord impressed my heart and said, 'You underestimate the power of your God.'" I then told them both what the Lord had me do. Anyway, what I am saying is that once we understand what God's faith can do, we won't doubt anything. Too many of us do err, not knowing the scriptures, nor the power of God (Matthew 22:29).

It is God's faith, God's power, and God's ability that spoke the world into existence. He spoke from the spiritual world and the physical world appeared the moment He spoke it into being. Faith's foundation is God's faith. The fact that we know that He will never change, when we ask for something, even if it seems impossible, we don't look at the natural. We look at God and His attributes, and we believe in His ability and His power to perform the prayer or petition asked of Him.

God has the faith to believe what seems impossible in the natural realm. God's soldiers must realize that the foundation of faith is God's faith that can do anything. Then when we are hindered by an obstacle, we will confront it and overcome it by faith in the power and ability of our God who can do the impossible!

Chapter 9

Obstacle: Faith's Freedom

> Then said Jesus to those Jews which believed on him, If ye continue in my word, then are ye my disciples indeed; And ye shall know the truth, and the truth shall make you free. They answered him, We be Abraham's seed, and were never in bondage to any man: how sayest thou, Ye shall be made free? Jesus answered them, Verily, verily, I say unto you, Whosoever committeth sin is the servant of sin. And the servant abideth not in the house for ever: but the Son abideth ever. If the Son therefore shall make you free, ye shall be free indeed (John 8:31–36).

THIS CHAPTER WILL REVEAL an obstacle that can hinder our overcoming by faith the most because faith's nemesis is hard at work here. Christ has set us free from sin, yet too many are chained or enslaved by sin. Some of us have allowed ourselves to be overcome by the lusts of the flesh, the lusts of the eye, or the pride of life and are not living in freedom from the bondage to sin. The freedom that Christ gave us becomes an obstacle because of sin. In other words, God's soldiers may never enjoy the freedom that faith in Christ offers. Instead of the freedom becoming a liberty, it becomes an obstacle because of self.

When Jesus says that if the Son makes you free, that free means to be liberated or delivered. The free indeed means to be unrestrained or not a slave to. Jesus wants us to know that we are free from the bondage of sin. Sin is natural to our old nature but the new nature in Christ is liberated from sin. We are no longer restrained, chained, or imprisoned by sin. In Christ, we are freed from its chains, its power, and its influence.

This chapter is vital to our understanding on how to confront and to overcome by faith. We must learn that the whole armor of God is the only way that we as God's soldiers can protect ourselves from the power of sin. The helmet of salvation protects our mind from wrong thoughts. The breastplate of righteousness protects us from wrong affections. Our loins girt with truth protects us against false teachings. The shield of faith will keep back the fiery darts of lies, sickness, lusts, etc. Then as we stand and do warfare through prayer asking the Holy Spirit to give us the strength to overcome the temptation trying to overcome us, the sword of the spirit which is the word of God will destroy whatever the devil tries to come at us with. As Jesus used the word of God, we must learn to be proficient in its use to send the devil packing (Matthew 4:3–10). Our thoughts and our affections are the key to living in the freedom that Christ has given us. They are what cause us to overcome the control of sin or be controlled by it.

Jesus says that if we continue in His word, we are His disciples indeed, we shall know the truth, and the truth shall make us free. Continue in the Greek means to abide, to dwell, to remain, and to endure. If we endure, meaning that we persist, suffer firmly, or patiently, we shall be freed. The truth will make us free from all that Christ's redemptive work on the cross delivered us from. However, we cannot know the truth unless we endure in His word. The question is what exactly is it that Christ's redemptive work has freed us from?

We know that it has freed us from the bondage or slavery of sin. Sin is to offend God. Whenever God's soldiers allow self to be the servants of sin, we live as slaves and not as a son or child of God enjoying all the benefits of sonship. A slave or servant is not free. Only the free, those Christ has liberated or delivered from sin, abide as a member of God's family. This will be more clarified as we go along in this chapter.

At present, we are trying to understand what being free is all about. Faith's birth is when we first experienced this freedom. That was when we realized that we were sinners or servants of sin, that we needed to confess our sins, that we needed to receive God's forgiveness, and that we needed to be delivered from sin. There was no doubt or unbelief. We experienced faith's freedom. It was such a rejuvenating experience to feel forgiven and cleansed from sin and its consequences.

After that, if we don't endure or abide in the word of God during tests, trials, storms, or obstacles, we can find ourselves back in bondage to some sin, any sin, even unbelief. What we must understand is that sin prohibits us from enjoying the freedom that faith in Christ has given us. What is freedom? It is liberation, emancipation, and independence. While we are slaves to sin, we are under its control. Christ's freedom emancipates or unshackles us from sin's control. We now have control over it. But freedom from sin is only the beginning of what the freedom in Christ involves.

Let's start to appreciate how much is involved in faith's freedom. Once God's soldiers comprehend the extent or the magnitude of it, it is an incredible revelation. But if we cannot overcome sin in our life, we cannot and will not experience faith's freedom. A servant or slave cannot enjoy the benefits of the children. The tragedy is that we allow ourselves to sin. It is we who yield to it.

> Likewise reckon ye also yourselves to be dead indeed unto sin, but alive unto God through Jesus Christ our Lord (Romans 6:11).

In faith's birth, we realized that we were spiritually dead because of sin, but God made us spiritually alive. At that time, we experienced a portion of faith's freedom. Jesus delivered us from being servants or slaves of sin. That gave us a taste of the freedom that Jesus has given us.

> Let not sin therefore reign in your mortal body, that ye
> should obey it in the lusts thereof (Romans 6:12).

Sin reigns in our body when we let or allow it. We yield to the desires or lusts of our flesh. Yet, John 8:36 informs us that sin doesn't have power over us. We have been delivered from its control through Christ. Only we can allow or let it have control over us. That's why Romans 6:12 says, *Let not sin therefore reign.* We must not allow or permit sin to control us. If we yield to sin, it will enslave us.

Jesus said that to follow Him, God's soldiers must deny self and take up our cross daily (Luke 9:23). If we deny ourselves, we give up ownership of self and give it to Christ. In other words, we cease to exist and depart from self. If we are to follow Jesus, we must give up all rights to our life. We give up the desires, the wants, the will of self, and live by the faith of Jesus Christ (Galatians 2:20). This is saying that we don't live for self, for self's desires, for self's wants, or for self's will; they have been crucified. We have given the rights to our life over to Jesus.

Now, let's focus on the difference between a servant and a member of God's family. John 8:35 says that a servant doesn't abide in the house forever, but the son abideth ever. What does that mean? It is saying that a servant or a slave can't abide in the house forever, because they have no family inheritance. Only a child is an official heir and inherits what belongs to the family.

As long as we struggle, allow ourselves to be a servant of sin, we cannot partake of the rights of the children. A servant doesn't participate in the family benefits. They are taken care of, but they don't have rights to whatever belongs to the family. We are either in bondage or slaves to sin or we are liberated and participating in the family benefits.

Christ has delivered God's soldiers from the control and power of sin. We have been freed, but if we choose to allow our members to be instruments of unrighteousness or sin, then we are again enslaved by sin. We are once again its servant.

Before continuing, let's make something clear. Not any of us has to be enslaved to sin. As we did in faith's birth, we confess our sin. God is faithful, He will forgive our sins, and He will cleanse us from all unrighteousness (1 John 1:9). Please understand that God is more eager to forgive us than we are to be forgiven. The whole plan of salvation proves that. God knows that as a slave or servant of sin, we cannot enjoy the liberty or the freedom that experiences all the rights of the children.

We must understand that sin stops us from enjoying those rights, because sin means to miss the mark or to not share in the prize. Sin in our life will bring chastisement, reprimand, and punishment from the Lord. God loves us too much and has done so much for us that He cannot allow us to stay in sin (Hebrews 12:6). He will do all that He can to encourage us back to Him and out of sin. Let's face it, no correction from the Lord is pleasant, but it is better to be corrected by Him, turn from our sin, and receive His blessings. Plainly put, disobedience brings misery and punishment. Obedience brings contentment and blessings.

Let me interject something here. Tests, trials, storms, and obstacles may seem like reprimand, but chastisement is only for those who willfully sin and who God must correct. If we find ourselves in sin and we confront it, we will overcome it by faith through confession and repentance.

It must be understood that God's obedient soldiers may have to confront many obstacles, but it has nothing to do with the chastisement for disobedience. Whatever we may have to confront is to instruct us in the use of God's armor. As God's soldiers there must always be the realization that we have a relentless enemy out to destroy us. He doesn't take a vacation from attacking us, and we must never take a vacation from using the whole armor of God. We must constantly make sure the helmet of salvation is protecting our mind from wrong thoughts. We must constantly make sure the breastplate of righteousness is protecting our heart from wrong affections. We must make sure our loins are girded with truth to protect us against false teachers, wrong doctrines, and all that is contrary to God's word. We must use of the shield of faith to protect ourselves from the devil's fiery darts of lies, sickness, etc. We must become proficient in the sword of the spirit which is the word of God that will cut to pieces any trap of the devil. We must always have our feet shod with the preparation of the gospel of peace to reconcile man to God. And to stay dressed in the armor, we must pray without ceasing to draw strength from the Lord and be enabled to stand against the obstacles that the enemy is trying to use to prevent us from overcoming.

Because Jesus liberated us from the power of sin. We are not only free from sin, but enjoy all that the servant of sin misses out on. How grievous must it be to God to see us not living as children free from sin and its consequences? To watch so many living below the family rights must grieve His Holy Spirit. Especially after what Jesus did to liberate us. The agony that God suffered to free us, and we live as slaves and servants to sin.

> Beloved, I wish above all things that thou mayest prosper
> and be in health, even as thy soul prospereth (3 John 2).

The Apostle John knew that the truth of faith's freedom should be part of our life. In John 8, he tells us that Jesus has freed us indeed. Then in 1 John 1:9, he tells us that this freedom means forgiveness and cleansing from sin. Now, in 3 John 2, he informs that this freedom includes every aspect of our life. This includes prosperity, physical health, and spiritual health.

It is God's will that His soldiers be freed from the power and control of sin, sickness, and poverty. Yes, there is a time to die, but sickness and poverty doesn't have control over us any more than sin does. Christ death has liberated us. Sometimes, God may give us a thorn in the flesh to keep us humble, but His grace will enable us to go on in spite of the thorn. It will not interfere with our work or life for Him. Paul was not hindered from performing his ministry for the Lord. If we glory in our thorn or infirmity and use it as an excuse to be remiss in our walk and work for Christ, it means that we are living below the grace of God.

Let me clarify this. Paul was buffeted or battered by this messenger of Satan, but he still wrote or narrated about half of the books in the New Testament. The Lord gave him the grace necessary to fulfill the ministry that God called him to perform.

Whatever God has called us to do, no thorn in our flesh can hinder it. When I was bed-ridden with my neck as told in my first book *Storms Are Faith's Workout*, I still ministered and prayed. No matter what the thorn may be, God will always give the grace to perform His ministry in our life.

How we live determines whether we are in chastisement or in blessings. If we don't hearken unto the voice of the Lord to obey Him, we will be chastised, punished, corrected, etc. (Hebrews 12:6). Sin has its negative consequences in our life. Whereas, living in the freedom from sin has its positive effects of blessings and promises from God.

What God's soldiers must also comprehend is that there will be trials, tests, storms, or obstacles that will come into our life. They have nothing to do with correction or chastisement, but we can count on the blessings and promises when in God's will. We may have to confront sickness, disease, financial hardship, doubt, confusion, anxiety, weariness, etc. But as long as we know that we are not in sin, we will use the armor of God to confront the obstacles and overcome them by faith. We will not believe any of the darts the enemy may use to tell us that God has forsaken us, that God doesn't love us, that God doesn't want to bless us, that God is trying to kill us, or that we have no rights to the family privileges, blessings, promises, etc.

Our freedom is first from sin, then freedom to enjoy all the promises that God has promised His children. As we endure in the word and don't give up, don't grow weary, don't give into unbelief, we stand in God's full armor, confront every obstacle, and overcome it by faith. Even in the darkest storms and facing giant obstacles, our needs will be met. Once we live in freedom from sin's control, we will experience all the blessings, all the promises of God that are our family rights!

Chapter 10

Obstacle: Faith's Rest

There remains therefore a rest for the people of God (Hebrews 4:9).

Come unto me, all ye that labour and are heavy laden, and I will give you rest. Take my yoke upon you and learn of me; for I am meek and lowly in heart: and ye shall find rest unto your souls. For my yoke is easy, and my burden is light (Matthew 11:28–30).

HOW CAN THERE BE an obstacle in faith's rest? This is quite easy to understand. Unless, we as God's soldiers are yoked up with the Lord, the burden becomes heavier the longer that we carry it. There is no rest when we are carrying or doing things in the flesh.

Before we continue, I want to help us understand that the rest in Hebrews 4:9 means a sabbatism. Figuratively it means the repose of Christianity as a type of heaven. The word rest in Matthew 11:28 means to repose, to refresh, and to rest. Rest in Matthew 11:29 means an intermission, by implying recreation or rest.

Webster's Dictionary 1828 dictionary defines recreation as refreshment of the strength and spirit after toil or relief from toil or pain; amusement in sorrow or distress. The main point is that faith's rest is a reprieve from the stress, the hardship, the toil, the battle, the storm, the obstacles, etc.

The previous chapters have listed various obstacles, and through them they help give us a foundation to build upon. God doesn't want His soldiers distraught and overwhelmed with the cares, the trials, the troubles, the storms, the obstacles, the politics, or the evils of this world. Our life is to be one that experiences faith's rest no matter what is going on in our life, the life of others, the world, the political arena, etc.

Jesus says, *Come unto to me, all ye that labour and are heavy laden.* This implies that we have a great load laid upon us, which we must carry to some place. Each step that we take is draining our strength, thereby making the load seem heavier. This is the way of our life. But if we go to Jesus, He promises us rest, that we will be refreshed, and that our load will be eased.

How can our load be eased? He says that if we take His yoke upon us. His *yoke* is that of faith in Him, in His ability, in His power, in His love, etc. If we can picture a traditional kitchen scale in our minds, that will help us to understand Christ's yoke. His *yoke* in the Greek means to join; the beam of a balance as connecting the scale. It is the beam that joins the pans on either side. One pan has the weights and the other pan has the load or that which is being weighed. Without the weights in the opposite pan, the load would drop.

The burdens of this life that could drain our strength and cause us to collapse under the load is balanced when we come to Jesus and take His yoke upon us. How is the load balanced? Verse 29 says, *Take my yoke upon you, and learn of me.* Jesus will teach God's soldiers how He balances the heavy load. Without Jesus, there is no beam to balance our load. Only as we yoke up with Christ is the load balanced and we find rest for our soul. We have to quit trying to carry things in our strength, in our knowledge, in our wisdom, in our education, etc.

The Greek says *rest* means to repose, to be refreshed, to have intermission, to have recreation. Yet, Webster's 1828 dictionary says *rest* is a quiet repose, a state of reconciliation to God, a state free from motion or disturbance.

Jesus tells us to *learn of me*. Now, that is telling us to learn the ways of Jesus or learn from His example. In *Storms Are Faith's Workout*, I used Mark 4:35–40 which shows us what rest in action looks like. The storm in Mark is a whirlwind, a tempest, or a violent storm. Now, a violent storm is definitely a disturbance. Yet, Webster's 1828 tells us that the rest that Jesus gives us is a state free from disturbance.

Now, Mark 4 informs us that while this disturbance, this tempest, this violent storm is raging Jesus slept. Yet, his disciples were in fear, terror, and panic. Let's think about that. When the tempest comes into our life, are we asleep with Jesus or are we panicking with the disciples?

Let's understand something here. When it says that Jesus was asleep, it means that Jesus was refreshing Himself during a violent storm. He wants God's soldiers to learn from Him. We need to learn how to rest or be refreshed no matter what is going on. We are to take recreation during the labor, the heavy loads, the storms, the trials of life, and the obstacles that must be overcome by faith.

Once God's soldiers learn to walk daily dressed in God's full armor, we will do as Jesus did and rest during the storm. If we understand the scale that was discussed earlier, we will comprehend what Jesus meant by taking His yoke upon us. What Jesus is saying to us is that He wants to be the balancing beam. He wants to be the one that connects the scales, or the one that is the balancer.

If we look at a scale and see that the two pans are balanced by the beam. On the left is the load and on the right is the weights. If we don't use the proper weights the load on the left tips the scale. In our life, that means we are overwhelmed, oppressed, worried, fearful, and feel undone. Our strength or our will to go on seems to be gone.

When this happens, we are like the disciples in the boat and feel that we are about to be destroyed. But according to Jesus, we are in this state because of unbelief (Mark 4:40). If we as God's soldiers have been learning from these obstacles, we should be asleep with Jesus in the boat. We should be experiencing faith's rest.

If we believe all that we have been taught concerning faith in the word of God, we will be asleep, resting, and being refreshed during the storm. In order to experience faith's rest, we must believe God and we must trust God.

Let's understand what rest is like. A baby rests in his mother's arms, contented, and totally trusting in mother to care, to protect, to feed, to love, to comfort, and to meet every need. The baby doesn't think about trusting; it comes naturally. The baby expects mommy to do it. That's what Jesus was doing in the boat. His faith in His Father to protect, etc. enabled Him to rest in that faith.

Now, what storm is raging in our life? Is it our children, our job, our finances, a sickness, an evil report? Whatever it is, Jesus said that He will balance it. His yoke is easy, and His burden is light.

Let's think about the scale again. The storm (whatever it may be) is on the left. Jesus is the beam that balances the two pans. Now, what does He use as the weight on the right to balance the load? It is quite simple. Jesus uses the word of God. Our knowledge of the word enables us to use whatever weight (promise, etc.) needed for Jesus to balance the load enabling us to live in a constant rest during whatever storm is raging.

This is an important factor that God's soldiers must comprehend. If we are using man's knowledge, man's wisdom, man's science, man's logic, man's medicine, etc. then our faith is in them. Our weight during any storm must be God's word. Only His word can balance the scale or the burden that we are carrying.

Let me interject a story here that happened many years ago. We were living in Iowa and my husband couldn't find work. Although pastoring a small church, there was no pay, and no parsonage. The church income was needed to support the church. Anyway, I was praying and looking out the parlor window at the street in the front of our house, and the devil said that's where you and all your belongings will be. I felt fear try to engulf me. But I immediately shook my head, and said, "No, but my God will supply all my need according to His riches in glory by Christ Jesus." I fell to my knees and cried, "Lord, I know the devil is a liar. You have not given me a spirit of fear, but of power, and of love, and of a sound mind." I felt that rest and peace that we are supposed to experience during the storm. When my husband came home, he had found a job. Plus, when the mail came in, someone had sent us a check that paid our bills, gave us grocery money, and gas money until my husband's first paycheck.

If I hadn't had on the armor and prayed the word of God, I probably would have been tossed about by fear like the disciples in the boat. That's why it is imperative that God's soldiers be constantly clothed in the full armor of God. The helmet of salvation will protect our mind from wrong thoughts, false doctrines, false teachers, the enemies lies, etc. As long as the helmet is in place, we then make sure the breastplate of righteousness is in place. The breastplate will protect our heart from wrong affections that are contrary to God's will.

What helps us to know what is the truth of God's will is having our loins girt with truth. Only the truth of God's word will enable us to discern what is false or lies. The shield of faith is to protect us from the fiery darts of the enemy. This is important in that his darts are full of malice, sickness, lies, etc. Then with prayer, we take the sword of the Spirit which is the word of God and destroy any snare the devil wields our way.

God doesn't want faith's rest to be an obstacle that we can't confront and overcome. In other words, it becomes an obstacle when the nemesis of faith causes us to listen to self and the devil's lies that we can't overcome, that we can't get through this, that this is more than we can handle, etc. Instead of a rest, we are in fear, turmoil, anxiety, doubt, etc. like the disciples in the boat when we should be sleeping with Jesus.

God wants His soldiers to enjoy faith's rest. It is the refreshment, the repose, the tranquility, the calm, etc. that faith in God, His word, and His ability enables us to experience when confronting obstacles in our life. Faith's rest is the balance that faith in God's word enables Jesus to give us during whatever obstacle the devil sends to destroy us!

Chapter 11

Obstacle: Faith's Satisfaction

> I beseech you therefore brethren by the mercies of God, that ye present your bodies a living sacrifice, holy, acceptable unto God which is your reasonable service. And be not conformed to this world: but be ye transformed by the renewing of your mind, that ye may prove what is that good, and acceptable and perfect will of God (Romans 12:1–2).

FAITH'S SATISFACTION CAN BE an obstacle to God's soldiers who have not learned to deny the nemesis of our faith (our flesh) and are not yielding to faith's mind or the mind of Christ. The word satisfaction in this chapter means the repose or contentment of the mind that results from the full gratification of desire. The repose means to rest in confidence.

Although we have revealed many obstacles to faith, I believe that they can be unlimited. Until we are perfected in His presence, we must see how much knowledge we lack. We have a great deal to learn.

If this scripture sounds familiar, that is because we used it in chapter seven concerning faith's mind. In that chapter, we saw the drastic change that takes place. We are metamorphosed from self thinking to Christ thinking. It is a great change like a caterpillar metamorphosing into a butterfly. But in this chapter, God's soldier must see something more than the caterpillar to butterfly.

The scriptures in Romans 12 reveal the response that we should make when considering the mercies of God. When we meditate upon what God has done for us, meaning His sacrificial death on the cross, we should be intreated to do what these verses implore us to do. If He could take our punishment, how much more should we present our bodies a living sacrifice, holy, and acceptable to God?

We understood that in faith's mind the transformation takes place in our mind. We must not be conformed and not be fashioned like the present age. God's soldiers must be transformed and live as people of the coming age or the next life with Christ.

God's mercy is the tenderness of heart which disposes God to overlook our sins and to forgive those sins. He does this, so the punishment is not what the law demands. We must comprehend that the law demands Hell for our sins.

I want to interject something here that I have found to be quite surprising. In my years of ministering, I have been amazed at the number of Christians that didn't believe that they deserve to go to Hell. Psalms 14:2–3 makes clear that when God looked down from heaven, He couldn't find one that did good or sought after Him. Romans 6:23 says that the wages of sin is death, but the gift of God is eternal life.

Wages is something that we earn. Since all have sinned according to Romans 3:23, we all have earned death. Divine justice is under obligation to give sinners their wages or that which they have earned. All that anyone of us has earned is death or Hell. But God's mercy, through the sacrifice of Christ, enables God to gift us with eternal life. However, we must understand the wages of sin is not eternal life, but eternal, spiritual death or Hell. The wages of sin is death is not referring to physical death.

> And it is appointed unto men once to die, but after this the judgment (Hebrews 9:27).

After we die physically is when we have the judgment. We either receive our wages of spiritual death, or we receive God's gift of eternal life. Although we learned much in faith's mind, faith's satisfaction is deeper and will give greater light, greater revelation, and greater understanding than faith's mind.

> For therein the righteousness of God is revealed from faith to faith: as it is written, The just shall live by faith (Romans 1:17).

We need to understand faith to faith. Let's look at the first grader. Can a first grader be expected or required to pass a fourth grader's test? Of course not, we know that we go from grade to grade. As we do, we gain more knowledge. More knowledge means that more is expected from us (Luke 12:48b).

That is what faith to faith is all about. Each grade, so to speak with its test should result in more knowledge, more understanding, etc. In this chapter, we should gain more knowledge or insight into Romans 12:1–2.

Why does the Apostle Paul use such a strong word of *beseech* which means to exhort, to advise, to caution, or to warn God's soldiers to offer, yield freely, or give our bodies as a living sacrifice accepted by God? The sacrifice here is not like the dead animals of the Old Testament, but it is living. It is our life. It is not a ritual activity like the Old Testament, but it is the involvement of our heart, our mind, and our will. In other words, it is our whole being. Since we have been given a free will, the choice is ours. Paul warned them to offer themselves freely to God without hesitation or reluctance.

> And he said unto them all, If any man will come after me, let him deny himself, and take up his cross daily, and follow me (Luke 9:23).

In chapter five, we learned that to deny self is to abstain, utterly disown, and depart from it. In other words, we give up our desires, our wants, our rights. We choose Christ's desires and Christ's wants unreservedly. If God's soldiers truly understand that self cannot count, but only Jesus and His will, we willingly give the right to our life over to Him.

If we do not deny self, we will never be transformed. We will remain conformed to this world. To be conformed means to be fashioned like or resemble the world. We will continue to have the morals of the world, the old nature, all that is opposite of pure Christianity. We will think, act, speak, and resemble the world. Our character, who we were before Christ is what people will hear and see. We must be transformed. In chapter seven, we learned that transformation is a metamorphosis; it is a drastic change or transfiguration.

The caterpillar to butterfly is an incredible transformation. The caterpillar crawls from place to place with several pairs of legs and has the shape and appearance of a worm. The butterfly flies from place to place with four wings and some are stunning with such color. When we think of it, it is sort of earthy to heavenly.

Let's look closer at the transformation. In Romans 12, the Apostle Paul advises, warns, or encourages us to freely give or present ourselves as a living sacrifice. One who abandons self and all its lusts of the eyes, lusts of the flesh, and the pride of life is freely presenting their bodies a living sacrifice.

Let's understand a little more about abandoning self. The caterpillar in order to be transformed into a butterfly has to abandon himself so to speak. Why do I say that? The caterpillar is never changed into a butterfly without its abandoning all rights to self. Have we really thought about what the caterpillar must do?

If the caterpillar is to be transformed or metamorphosed, it must spin or weave an adequate cocoon or protective covering. If the cocoon is not weaved, the next process can't take place. The caterpillar doesn't turn itself into a butterfly. However, once in the cocoon, then nature can do the transformation.

In order to be transformed from spiritual death into spiritual life as in chapter one, we must want the change. We must weave a cocoon, so-to-speak, with the word of God. Only the word can renew our mind, which then allows God to transform us from the old nature into the new nature or from spiritual death to spiritual life. As the cocoon or protective covering allows nature to transform the caterpillar into a butterfly, the word which is our cocoon or protective covering changes our morals, our thought pattern, etc. Through the change, our mind is renewed. It is totally renovated which allows God to transform us from death to life which is the old nature to the new nature.

We will never be transformed without yielding or giving up our rights to self. We must choose and desire to no longer be the worldly-minded caterpillar, but we must choose and desire to be the heavenly minded butterfly. Unless we want to please God and to be what He wants, we will never be transformed.

In this chapter, it is imperative that we choose not to be fashioned like the world but be transformed into the likeness of Christ by our minds being renewed or renovated. The old destructive, depraved, and decayed thought patterns or beliefs must be renewed, renovated, and made new after decay in order to be transformed.

Why is it imperative that we be transformed or metamorphosed by the renewing of our mind. As we learned in chapter seven, it is imperative that God's soldiers have the mind of Christ. The Apostle Paul knew how vital it is for our mind to be renewed and that's why he warns, cautions, and exhorts us to freely give up self and be transformed.

Romans 12 makes clear that if we are not transformed by the renewing of our mind, we will not be able to prove, discern, distinguish, understand, or to know the will, the purpose, and the desire of God. What this is teaching is that if we don't know God's will, we have not allowed God to transform us. We do not have the renewed mind or the mind of Christ. We are trying to hold onto something that God wants gone out of our life. We may love something or someone more than God. We may not have forgiven someone. We may be desiring that which will lead us astray. In other words, if we are not truly a living sacrifice, not renewing our mind with God's word, not allowing Him to transform us, we will not know His will or what He wants us to do.

The Apostle Paul knew that the only way to know God's will is to freely give up self. This means that we give our life back to

God and allow Him through His word and the power of the Holy Spirit to change our morals, our thought patterns, and transform us into the new creation that is no longer earth confined. In order to be renewed, God's soldiers must live Galatians 2:20 where it is no longer us that live but Christ living in us. That means that we no longer live to self but to God.

Obstacle: Faith's Satisfaction is meant to reveal that we can know and understand His will, His plan, and His direction for our life if we give up all rights to self. It cannot be what we want, what we think, or what we desire, but what God wants, what God thinks, and what God desires.

We must come to Him as the caterpillar and willingly spin our cocoon by reading, believing, and studying His word. As our mind is renewed, we allow Him to transform us into the butterfly. In other words, we will become a new creation without any evidence of the old.

Let me say that it is all beyond me how He does it. I mean how He transforms us from spiritual death to spiritual life. But now, He wants us to know that we can know His will for us. He not only wants to transform us into something beautiful, but to know without any doubt what His will is.

In this chapter, God is revealing that as we know His will, we will know His desire to bless, to heal, to protect us. We will know the mind or the thinking of God for our life so that we, like Jesus, can always do what pleases the Father (John 8:29).

> Can two walk together, except they be agreed (Amos 3:3)?

To be agreed means to be in harmony or to be of one mind. In chapter seven, we used Philippians 2:5 which states that we are to let the mind of Christ be in us. The key in that verse was to *let* which means to allow to, don't prevent, or forbid. We must allow the mind or the thinking of Christ to enter into our mind.

In this chapter, we offer ourselves or freely give up all rights to self and let God have His way. This then allows His thinking to be our thinking. As we do that, God reveals His will to us. However, it must be understood, that reading His word without rightly dividing it will cause us to be led astray. Remember, the devil quoted scripture, but in every instance, it was not rightly divided. That's why Jesus came back each time with the rightly divided word (Matthew 4:3–10).

The main point that God's soldiers must learn is that if we believe that something is God's will and it goes against scripture as a whole, it is not God's will. Let's look at few examples to understand this. We have diabetes and we ask if we can have a piece of chocolate cake. We may hear that we can, but we know that chocolate cake is like poison to our system. What we have just done is abuse or defile the temple of the Holy Ghost (1 Corinthians 3:17). If we know someone is not saved and we date them, go into business with them, or yolk up in marriage, we again have disobeyed the word of God (2 Corinthians 6:14).

What we must learn is that if it is contrary to scripture (we are the temple of the Holy Ghost; be not unequally yoked together with unbelievers, etc.), it is not God's will. Only as we willingly give up all rights to our thoughts, our ways, our will, our life can we be in harmony with and of one mind with God. As we live Romans 12:1–2, we will not only walk in one mind with the Lord, but we will know His will for our life.

I will interject another example here. There was something that I felt that I needed, and I prayed. I heard the Lord impress my heart that I did not need it. I was puzzled, because I really thought it was a need. But my heart was impressed with the question if I wanted God's will or my will. I immediately submitted to the Lord and thanked Him for direction. We must be willing to deny self at all times. If we don't, we will walk in our will and not the Lord's.

At this point, let's again look at the definition that was given for satisfaction at the beginning of the chapter. It said that satisfaction is the repose or contentment of mind which results from the full gratification of desire.

Let me help us to understand that definition. My greatest desire is to know God's will and to freely accept it without hesitation and without question. As I willingly accept His will, I am in complete harmony, of one mind, and in total agreement with God. Then, my mind is content and resting in the confidence that God's will for my life will be accomplished.

There is no satisfaction of spirit in this life, unless we desire of our own free-will to be one with God which is to be of one mind with Him. Only as God's soldiers do Romans 12:1–2 can we do Amos 3:3. To walk with God is to agree with Him. This means total satisfaction because our mind or thinking is the thinking of Christ. We can only do that as we are clothed in the full armor of God. The helmet of salvation protects our thoughts. The breast-plate of righteousness protects our affections. Our loins girt with truth enables us to know what is of God and what is of the devil. The shield of faith will protect us from any of the lying darts from Satan to gain entrance. The sword of the Spirit which is the word of God will quench and annihilate the enemies fiery darts. Prayer will keep us in tune with God and His will.

Because I was clothed in God's armor, I could be completely satisfied when the Lord said that I didn't need what I thought I needed. If I needed it, He would have supplied it. What must be understood is that when we have the thought patterns of Christ, our mind is free of doubt, worry, anxiety, uncertainty, etc. However, we can only be of one mind with God as we remain fully clothed in His armor. If we allow the devil's lies to enter our mind, we could entertain them and doubt God, His word, and His ability. As we remain in an attitude of prayer or constant communication with God, we will stand by faith using the sword of the Spirit which is the word of God. The word will cut to pieces the devil's darts, and by faith, we will overcome the obstacle.

What could be more fulfilling or more satisfying for God's soldiers than to be in harmony with Him? As we renounce all rights to self, the thinking of Jesus enables us to know and walk in the will of God!

Chapter 12

Obstacle: Faith's Secret

Let us hold fast the profession of our faith without wavering; for he is faithful that promised (Hebrews 10:23).

IN ORDER TO UNDERSTAND the obstacle in this chapter, we
will look more closely at the scripture reference. The word *profession* is an open declaration or acknowledgment of one's belief.
Faith in this scripture means an anticipation, an expectation, a
confidence, or hope. *Without wavering* means not leaning, firm,
or resolute.

Let us hold fast the profession of our faith without wavering is
saying that we are to be firm or steadfast in our declaration or acknowledgment of our faith or expectation in God. We are to keep
in our memory, hold on tight to our anticipation, our expectation,
and our confidence in God. What we must understand is that it
means holding on even during severe physical pain. Jacob wrestled
all night with the angel of the Lord while in agonizing pain, but he
did not let go until he was blessed (Genesis 32:24–30).

The last part of the verse reveals why we hold fast. *For he
is faithful that promised* means that He is trustworthy, sure, and
true. The word *promised* is telling us that the promise of God is
the declaration or assurance which God has given in His word

of bestowing blessings on His people. This assurance rests on the perfect justice, power, benevolence, and immutable veracity of God. The veracity or truth of God is immutable; it is not capable of change. Whatever God promises will not change. Any alteration is impossible. God cannot change, and He never will.

So far in this chapter, we are learning that we must not allow anything to prevent us from holding on to our hope in God or our expectations from Him. We must always be expecting from God (Hebrews 11:6). In other words, as long as we hang on, we will receive the blessings or promises that He promised.

God's soldiers must not doubt the declarations, His promises no matter what we see in the natural.

> To everything there is a season, and a time to every pur-
> pose under the heaven (Ecclesiastes 3:1).

The word *season* refers to an appointed occasion or an appointed time. *Time* means a set period. *Purpose* denotes for design to resolve, to determine the end, or the accomplishment. This is saying that God has determined certain things to particular times, and a time or season for its accomplishment. He has given everything its time, its cycle, its season according to His design and His will.

This reveals to us that we are subjected to times and changes ordained by God. He predetermines all of life's activities. However, God has not predetermined the evil that man's free-will does. Because God has foreknowledge of their evil, He can use it to work His design for those who are His children. The last part of the verse, *under the heaven,* is anything that is subjected to time. Heaven does not have a time frame or seasons.

As I've ministered through the years, I have taught many times that there is a time frame from the time of God's promise until the manifestation of the promise. Now, as we think about seasons, we think of our four seasons of winter, spring, summer, and fall. And we understand that God ordained each season to have a certain time and a certain purpose. Different things take place or occur during each season (Genesis 8:32). Thus, all the seasons with their purpose, their design, or their goal are needed to complete the whole.

If we think of planting crops, there is a time to till the ground, a time to sow, a time to water, and a time to reap. There is no sowing a seed of anything and reaping or harvesting the next day. Everything has a season or a time. There is a time to be born and a time to die, a time to plant and a time to pluck up that which was planted, a time to weep and a time to laugh, a time to mourn and a time to dance, a time to keep and a time to cast away, a time to keep silence and a time to speak, etc. (Ecclesiastes 3:1–8).

Okay, let's understand how different some of these seasons or times are. There is a big difference between being born and dying or between weeping and laughing. If we look at the seasons in nature of winter, spring, summer, and fall, we see how distinctive they can be. Some of us prefer one season over another. I personally do not enjoy winter with the cold and ice. However, I have no problem with the other three.

Well, that is what our life here is. The different times or seasons in our life have the same effect. Some seasons are uncomfortable on our flesh. We don't like weeping, but we enjoy laughing. But without all the seasons or times in our life, God cannot accomplish His design or His plan for our life.

In the previous chapter, we learned that we can know God's will and walk in harmony with Him. In this chapter, God wants us to see and think as He does. He wants us to take the knowledge from chapter eleven and walk in harmony with Him no matter the season.

> Not that I speak in respect of want: for I have learned, in whatsoever state I am, therewith to be content (Philippians 4:11).

We quote that verse often, but do we understand what the Apostle is saying? He is telling us that he did not concern himself with what he wanted. He had left that responsibility to God who promises to take care of all his needs through Christ Jesus (Philippians 4:19).

Paul knew that the greatest contentment or satisfaction is knowing God's will and walking in harmony with God. What God's soldiers must understand is that God doesn't want us to look at the seasons of our life as good or bad times.

> And we know that all things work together for good to them that love God, to them who are the called according to his purpose (Romans 8:28).

All things, all seasons, and all times are working out the purpose or the design of God for good to those who love Him. To help us understand, let's consider again the planting of a crop. We know it is not an overnight endeavor. There is toil and sweat before there is the benefit of the fruit or harvest. If we get tired of the toil and sweat and feel as if we'll never reap, and just give up, we will not harvest a crop.

In this chapter, we must understand that faith is perpetual, never-ending, continuous, everlasting, and eternal. God's faith spoke all things into existence and His faith is part of eternity. His faith is forever. It is God's faith that upholds all things by the word of His power (Hebrews 1:3).

> But let him ask in faith, nothing wavering. For he that wavereth is like a wave of the sea driven with the wind and tossed. For let not that man think that he shall receive any thing of the Lord (James 1:6–7).

We cannot have faith or believe God about a promise today and tomorrow allow a season to put doubt or unbelief in our heart. We have to hold fast, to be steadfast, and to be firm in our trust and belief in God. We must do as Jacob did and hang on with all that we have to God and keep our memory fresh with that expectation, anticipation, and confidence in God until the promise is fulfilled. It is a matter of continuous prayer and persevering through whatever season fully clothed in God's armor.

During the winter, we look out in our natural eyes and all seems dead. It appears as if life is forsaken. But the eyes of faith know that under that snow and ice, new life is earnestly waiting to spring forth. Certain seasons or times in our life can be very trying. It is during those seasons that we must be very vigilant. If God's soldiers are not fully armed in the full armor of God and persevering in prayer, the devil walking around as a roaring lion will devour us (1 Peter 5:8).

In the *Chronicles of Narnia: The Silver Chair* by C. S. Lewis, published by Geoffrey Bles in 1953, Prince Rillian overcome by the death of his mother, gave place to the devil. In giving the enemy place, he became a prisoner in the deep realm of unbelief. He forgot the sunlit land and thought the deep realm was reality. Yes, he was delivered, but not all get out of the deep realm and again see the sunlit land.

That's why it is imperative to make sure the helmet of salvation is on to protect the mind from false doctrines, wrong thoughts, lies, etc. We must also make sure the breastplate of righteousness is in place to protect our heart from wrong affections that could lead us away from the truth of Christ and His word. The shield of faith must be used so that we don't allow unbelief to enter into our life. As we persevere in prayer and use the sword of the Spirit or the word of God, we will destroy any obstacles of the enemy. If Prince Rillian had been clothed in the armor of God, he would not have allowed himself to be deceived by the enemy. Only as God's soldiers are constantly clothed in the full armor of God can we stay out of the deep realm of unbelief.

Depression, desires, or the flesh will take over if we forget our anticipation, our expectation, or our confidence in God's promises. If the devil can get us to doubt, he will bring us down into the deep realm of unbelief. Without continuous faith in God, in His ability, and in His word, we could end up in the deep realm and lose our promised blessing like Israel in the wilderness. We must understand that seedtime (the promise) until harvest (the blessing) will take time. During the waiting is when the devil will use his arsenal of weapons to discourage us. Only the armor will prevent us from entertaining or meditating upon his lies.

There is a time or a season for God to fulfill His promise. If we are in the deep realm of unbelief during the harvest time, we will miss out. If we are in unbelief when we are to be in faith, we will receive nothing from God (James 1:6–7). I know that is a hard saying, but the Lord wants us to grasp hold of the importance of faith in this chapter. If we have never understood it before, it's time for God's soldiers to grasp hold of its necessity and importance..

> Be not deceived; God is not mocked: for whatsoever a man soweth, that shall he also reap (Galatians 6:7).

This makes clear that whatever we plant, we will reap or harvest. This is a promise from God. He is not man that He can lie (Numbers 23:19).

In this chapter, we must look at it in reference to faith versus unbelief. Our foundation scripture of Hebrews 10:23 says to hold fast our profession of faith without wavering, for God is faithful to fulfill His promise.

If we are sowing faith by seizing and holding fast to our promise and not allowing anything to cause us to waver, we will harvest or reap that promise. But if we allow ourselves to waver and sow unbelief, we will reap or harvest no promise from God. James makes clear that the person that wavers will receive nothing from God.

Sowing faith reaps the fruit of faith. That means that we receive whatever God promised. If we sow unbelief, we reap the fruit of unbelief which receives nothing from God. If we think of that thought or reality, it can be quite sobering. It should cause us to stop, to think, and to re-evaluate our faith walk.

I understand that different seasons of trials, grief, financial difficulties, sickness, etc. can be difficult. Yet, the Apostle Paul said in Philippians that he had learned to be content or satisfied in all seasons. Now, think about this. He claimed that the seasons of satisfaction or contentment included being abased which means that he had been reduced to a low state and degraded. He had suffered being hungry to the point of starvation. Then in 2 Corinthians 11:24–28, Paul says he had been beaten, stoned, in perils of waters, in perils of robbers, in weariness, painfulness, hunger, thirst, cold, and nakedness, etc.

In all that Paul confronted on his faith journey, he had learned the secret of being content in whatever the season. According to Webster's Dictionary the word *secret* means properly separate, hid, concealed from the notice or knowledge of all persons except the individual or individuals concerned. In other words, it's something hidden from all but the one or ones the secret concerns.

> The secret things belong unto the Lord our God: but those things which are revealed belong unto us and to our children forever; that we may do all the words of this law (Deuteronomy 29:29).

Something that is revealed means it is disclosed, discovered, or made known from Heaven. God has been pleased to reveal His will to man. He reveals His will through revelation of His word, impressing our heart, by a check in our spirit to stop us, etc.. We know from chapter eleven that we can know God's will.

Now, what is the secret of being content in all the seasons of our life? How could Paul be satisfied being hungry, beaten, stoned, shipwrecked, etc.? In chapter five, we learned that we must live Luke 9:23 and deny ourselves, take up our cross daily, and follow Jesus. We understand that to deny self is to utterly disown or separate from self. That means that we no longer count. We don't think about what we need. Whatever we need is left up to God to supply.

If satisfaction or complete fulfillment is knowing God's will and being in harmony with Him, then we have discovered the secret of faith. Faith's secret is accepting every season and being satisfied or content in it, because we are in God's will. If we desire God's will for our life, there will be uncomfortable seasons on our flesh. Contentment is not contingent upon the season, but it is knowing that we are in God's will.

Because God's soldiers deny self the lust of the flesh, the lust of the eyes, and the pride of life, we are content with God's will. We cherish walking in harmony with Him. What we remember is that all seasons contain God's promise. In other words, He hasn't taken it back. That's why it is imperative that we don't look at the hardship, trial, etc. of the season. If we look at the obstacle, we will grow weary and quit.

The expectation of the promise first experienced at the conception or revelation of the promise must be seized. We must hold on tight to the promise knowing that God is faithful. The secret of faith is giving no place to allow doubt or unbelief. It is wrestling all night even when you are in excruciating pain from a dislocated hip, so to speak.

We must understand that it is God's will for us to harvest or reap every promise He has given. That's why He encourages us to hold fast the profession of our faith without wavering until we reap. The secret of faith can be an obstacle if we have not learned to be content in all situations. In other words, we are not comfortable being in God's will because it is difficult on our flesh. That's why we must learn to deny self it's way in our life. Once we have learned to keep self under the submission to God's will, we will have the victory no matter what season. God's soldiers know that the secret of faith is being content in all seasons, because each one is the will of God to accomplish His design for our life!

Chapter 13

Obstacle: Faith's Impediment

> Wherefore seeing we also are compassed about with so great a cloud of witnesses, let us lay aside every weight, and the sin which doth so easily beset us, and let us run with patience the race that is set before us (Hebrews 12:1).

AN IMPEDIMENT IS A hindrance or obstruction in doing something. That means that our faith can have an obstacle that obstructs the progress of faith's journey. If God's soldiers understand this impediment, they will be enabled to overcome it.

Our scripture in Hebrews says that we are compassed about with so great a cloud of witnesses. The word *compassed* means that we are encircled or enclosed. If we are surrounded with a circle, we are enclosed like in an arena. *Cloud of witnesses* refers to a great number of martyrs which means a great number of people that give testimony or evidence. All these people can attest or affirm to something being true or genuine.

Every weight implies a burden or hindrance. A hindrance is an impediment that stops progression or advance. *The sin* is from two Greek words meaning offence which implies to miss the mark and so not share in the prize. The word *beset* means to thwart a racer in every direction. To thwart meant to oppose, hence, to frustrate or to defeat. *With patience* means constancy, endurance, or a patient continuance. This means to stay under, to remain or to undergo or bear trials and to have fortitude under suffering. *Race* in this verse means a contest, an effort or anxiety. It is a conflict, a contention, or a fight. A conflict is a struggling with difficulties; it is a striving to oppose or to overcome.

This struggling is of the mind against an opposition of forces. What we must comprehend is that the race in Hebrews 12:1 is a struggle to resist and to overcome the opposition (whatever it may be) against our mind or our thinking. This illuminates that without the helmet of salvation, God's soldiers will not be empowered to resist the forces against our mind.

The opening scripture in this chapter alludes to the Olympic games. Let me explain something about the games. All the contenders were aware that the eyes of the principal men were fixed upon them and they were induced, influenced, and encouraged to give all they had. They would force or strain their bodies to the limit. In other words, they would push themselves beyond what they were capable of to please those watching.

What Paul is saying in Hebrews 12:1 is that the cloud of witness, that great group that is encircled around us, should encourage us to go beyond our limit. Hebrews chapter eleven tells us that the cloud of witnesses are the heroes of faith. It names Abel, Enoch, Abraham, Sarah, Isaac, Jacob, Joseph, Moses, Joshua, Rahab, etc. However, the cloud of witnesses is all who have confronted the obstacles on faith's journey and overcame them by faith. In other words, they ran the race and crossed the finish line. Because of their faith, we are to be encouraged by those who made it. As we see what they endured, our spirit is lifted and encouraged. It gives us revived strength to continue our race.

In this chapter we will learn the burdens, the hindrances, or the obstacles that could become impediments that stop our progression, our advancing, or that which impedes our going forward. It is essential in this chapter to understand why all weights must be laid aside. All weights that hinder, obstruct, or burden must not become an impediment. We alone let them become an impediment when we allow the weights to become too heavy.

We must lay aside all that hinders, obstructs, or burdens us. It is imperative that we overcome by faith all that interferes with our race. Our eyes must constantly be on the prize and not the obstacle that we are facing or the season we are in.

> By faith Noah, being warned of God of things not seen as yet, moved with fear, prepared an ark to the saving of his house; by the which he condemned the world, and became heir of the righteousness which is by faith (Hebrews 11:7).

Noah is one of the heroes of faith that made it. Yet, we read about the ark in Genesis and think, what overcoming is that? What kind of race did he overcome? But if we read Genesis 6:5, we see that the evil in man was only evil continuously. Let's think about that. Noah was living amongst all that wickedness and yet he found grace in the eyes of the Lord.

All of mankind except for Noah, his wife, his three sons, and his three daughters-in-law came through the flood. Only eight people amongst a multitude of whoremongers, thieves, adulterers, fornicators, murderers, blasphemers of God, etc. were to enter the ark and be saved from the flood.

Now, Noah was five-hundred years old when told to build the ark. That means that he had been under or subjected to the burden, the influence, the hindrance, the obstacle of a people that God said that the thoughts of this people are only evil continually for five-hundred years. Then for the next one-hundred years, he builds the ark. According to 2 Peter 2:5, during that time, he was a preacher of righteousness to that ungodly world.

That tells us that Noah must have put up with incredible ridicule and mockery the whole time he was building the ark. The whole race of people who did not believe in God surrounded Noah. Can we fathom the daily torment? He had to have wickedness trying to destroy his faith day after day. However, it wasn't a day, a week, a month, a year, ten years, twenty years, or fifty years, it was one-hundred years. That is the length of time it took him to finish the task of building, stocking, and entering the ark.

We must understand that it was not only the spiritual burden or fatigue of the evil oppression all around, but the physical burden or fatigue of building the ark, gathering all the animals, fowls, the food, water, etc. that would be needed. The other point is that it had not rained as of yet on the earth. Noah had never seen rain or a flood (Hebrews 11:7).

How many of us would have built an ark when we never heard of a flood? That alone could have hindered Noah, but he didn't lean on his own understanding and try to figure it out. He had no idea what rain or a flood was. But by faith, he built the ark. Noah obeyed God without comprehending what a flood was.

We can be assured that each day this evil people were there to ridicule and mock him. If we think about it, we can see people deriding him. "Look everyone Noah's gone off his rocker, he's building a boat that floats on sand." "Well, I heard he and his sons are going to push it across the dessert to the ocean." "No, you have it all wrong. He says his God is going to do it." Whatever ridicule that Noah encountered, it had to have been trying on him and his family. Imagine one-hundred years of this day after day with people constantly mocking and laughing.

At this time, we will look at another hero of faith who is not named in Hebrews chapter eleven.

> Because all those men which have seen my glory, and
> my miracles, which I did in Egypt and in the wilderness,
> and have tempted me now these ten times, and have not
> hearkened to my voice; Surely they shall not see the land
> which I sware unto their fathers, neither shall any of them
> that provoked me see it: But my servant Caleb, because
> he had another spirit with him, and hath followed me
> fully, him will I bring into the land whereinto he went;
> and his seed shall possess it (Numbers 14:22–24).

While I was seeking the Lord about this chapter, I wanted someone else to list as a hero of faith that we could relate to. It had to be someone different from the usual listed in the heroes of faith. The Lord reminded me of Caleb who I had preached about as being just a regular man of God. He was like any man or woman whose faith in God made the difference.

Let's look at Caleb and his faith. He was one of those delivered out of Egypt. When Moses chose the twelve spies to spy out the land, he was one of them (Numbers 13:6). Then in Numbers 13:26–33, we find that all the twelve spies agreed that the land was rich and flowing with milk and honey. However, ten of the spies gave an evil report and claimed it was impossible to go up against a people who were giants.

In Numbers 14:6–9, both Joshua and Caleb rent their clothes and beg the people not to rebel against the Lord nor fear the people of the land. What made them claim that not going into the land would be rebellion against God? Let's look at some more scriptures for the answer.

> And the Lord said, I have surely seen the affliction of my people which are in Egypt, and have heard their cry by reason of their taskmasters; for I know their sorrows; And I am come down to deliver them out of the hand of the Egyptians, and to bring them up out of that land unto a good land and a large, unto a land flowing with milk and honey; unto the place of the Canaanites, and the Hittities, and Amorites, and the Perizzites, and the Hivites, and the Jubusites (Exodus 3:7–8).

> And the Lord said unto Moses, Depart, and go up hence, thou and the people which thou hast brought up out of the land of Egypt, unto the land which I sware unto Abraham, to Isaac, and to Jacob, saying, Unto thy seed will I give it: And I will send an angel before thee; and I will drive out the Canaanite, the Amorite, and the Hittite, and Perizzite, the Hivite, and the Jebusite (Exodus 33:1–2).

Moses had made this all known, for the spies all claimed that it is surely a land that floweth with milk and honey. So it is quite clear that they knew that God had not only promised a land flowing with milk and honey, but that He would send an angel to drive out the inhabitants.

Anyway, we see the people refuse to listen to Joshua and Caleb and were about to stone them. If the glory of the Lord had not appeared to stop them, they would have stoned both Joshua and Caleb to death. Now, God is angry with the people and informs Moses that He would smite them with pestilence, disinherit them, and they would not see the promise land (Numbers 14).

God promises that His servant Caleb, because he had another spirit with him, and had followed God fully, would be brought into the land that he had spied out. He would not only inherit it, but his seed was also to possess it (Numbers 14:24). Then in Numbers 14:29–30, God promised that all twenty years old and upward would die in the wilderness, except Joshua and Caleb.

This is important to this chapter concerning faith's impediment. Caleb is definitely over twenty years of age. Yet, he is promised an inheritance in the land where he was one of the twelve spies. Of course, we all know that after this, God said that they would all wander in the wilderness one year for each of the forty days that the spies spied out the land (Numbers 14:34). That means that they had to wander in the wilderness for forty years without a place to call home.

Let's not forget that Caleb was surrounded by this people that murmured, complained, and had continuous unbelief. Yet, he ran the race for the whole wilderness wandering and never complained or murmured. He never joined the crowd going in the opposite direction of God.

At this point, I want to show something about Noah and Caleb so that we begin to understand what the obstacle in faith's impediment is. First of all, both Noah and Caleb had been given a promise. Noah's promise is in Genesis chapter six where we see that the whole earth was evil. Only Noah found grace in the eyes of the Lord and the Lord informs him that He would destroy all flesh that has breath on the earth.

God then tells him that He would establish His covenant with Noah and that he, his wife, his sons, and their wives would all enter the ark. God promises to preserve or save Noah and his family, but it takes one-hundred years before they would enter the ark. That means it was a hundred years of believing and waiting for God to fulfill His promise while living among a multitude of mocking unbelievers. That's the kind of faith that God's soldiers must have to overcome in His armor.

Now, let's look at Caleb and his promise. In Numbers 14:24, God promised Caleb an inheritance in the land where he went. Then after the years of wandering and fighting the inhabitants, Caleb comes to Joshua and asks for his inheritance that God through Moses promised. He says that he was forty years old when he went in as a spy, and it is now forty-five years later.

Caleb waited for forty-five years without wavering. Forty years wandering in the wilderness and five years subduing the promise land. But he continued in the faith believing God and he received the promise. That's the kind of steadfastness that God's soldiers must have to overcome in His armor.

Let's look again at our scripture verse in Hebrews at the beginning of this chapter. It is imperative that God's soldiers understand this scripture to overcome the obstacle of faith's impediment. In the scripture reference, it says the sin which doth so easily beset us. According to the Greek, the word *sin* in this verse means to miss the mark and not share in the prize. We all know that unbelief is what kept the Israelites out of the promise land, and unbelief caused the evil multitude from being saved from the flood.

Unbelief is the sin that will cause us to lose the race of faith or miss the mark. But God wants His soldiers to understand how unbelief or a lack of faith comes about. It is the weights which are burdens, hindrances, worries, etc. that become impediments and stop progression of our faith journey.

Let us understand these weights that can become impediments. How many of us today will stand firm in the faith with people laughing, mocking, ridiculing, etc. day in and day out? But the weights didn't hinder Noah. He took it for a hundred years. No impediment here.

How many Christians today will stand firm in the faith when ten out of twelve are saying the opposite? Then what we are saying causes people to get so angry that our life is in danger. Not only are the people wanting to kill you, but because of their sin, you have to spend forty years in the wilderness wandering and wandering and wandering. Yet, Caleb wasn't weighed down to unbelief. He believed God's promise and ran the race to receive it. No impediment here.

Are God's soldiers running the race or are the weights becoming impediments hindering our journey of faith? What we must remember is that all promises have a time factor. We receive the promise, then comes the testing, the trial, the storm, or the obstacle of our faith like Noah and Caleb. It is the time that we had better make sure the whole armor of God is on and we know how to use it. If we have not become proficient in the full armor, this is the time that the weights can become impediments that shake our faith.

If we have learned that the helmet of salvation will protect our mind from lies, false doctrines, or evil reports, we will not allow anything contrary to God's truth to enter into our thoughts. The breastplate of righteousness if in place will keep our heart from any devotion or affection that is contrary to loving God with all our heart, with all our soul, and with all our mind (Matthew 22:37). Our loins girt with the truth of God's word enables us to recognize wrong doctrines and to perceive where the devil lies in wait to deceive us. As we persevere in prayer and wield the sword of the Spirit which is the word of God, we will put to naught any attempt by the devil to trip us up (Matthew 4:1–11). Of course, the shield of faith will protect the rest of the armor. Once we are firm in our faith, we will be able to quench all the fiery darts of the enemy by faith.

If God's soldiers are not fully dressed in the whole armor of God, the enemy's darts will get through to our mind. From our mind, things get into our heart. If we happen to miss a dart with the shield or the sword, the helmet of salvation will protect our mind from false doctrines, lies, and evil reports. As long as we stop them from entering into our mind, they will be prevented from entering our heart where we could find ourselves devoted to something contrary to God.

Why do we receive a promise and immediately comes the trial of our faith, the examination, the storm, or the obstacle?

> Wherein ye greatly rejoice, though now for a season, if need be, ye are in heaviness through manifold temptations: That the trial of your faith, being much more precious than of gold that perisheth, though it be tried with fire, might be found unto praise and honour and glory at the appearing of Jesus Christ (1 Peter 1:6–7).

Heaviness in the Greek is a distress, a sorrow, a grief. Now, I believe that would be a weight that could become an impediment for sure. The word *temptations* means to test, to try, to prove, to examine. In other words, it is the storms and obstacles that the enemy ambushes us with to cause us to quit the race.

In chapter two, we learned that our faith is examined to see if it is genuine. Does our faith have sufficient strength? Like I revealed in *Storms Are Faith's Workout: Preparing Christians for Spiritual Ambush*, trials or storms are the only way to strengthen our faith. As a body builder keeps lifting weights to build up his muscles, our trials, storms, or obstacles are weights to build up our faith.

The verse in first Peter makes clear that the trials are to make our faith give praise, honor, and glory to Jesus. We must be tested, must have storms, or obstacles to see if our faith is genuine or will the weight become the impediment that leads to unbelief. Yet, how many of us are rejoicing in God, His ability, His word during these trials, these tests, these examinations, these storms, these obstacles of burdens, sorrows, finances, etc. that are weights that could become impediments that hinder our journey of faith?

In this chapter, God's soldiers must ask if the tests, the trials, the burdens, the sorrows, the storms, the obstacles, or the weights are strengthening our faith? Have they become impediments hindering our race or journey of faith? Are they interfering with our faith?

We learned in chapter ten concerning faith's rest that the balance beam and the weight of God's word should balance our heavy load. However, in this chapter concerning faith's impediment the weight is the heavy load that can become an impediment that destroys or weakens our faith.

Let's consider the weights of Noah and the weights of Caleb. Both are part of the cloud of witnesses that are to encourage and strengthen our faith to lay aside those weights, those burdens, those sorrows, those finances, those griefs, those infirmities, etc. that could turn into faith's impediment and hinder, weaken, or destroy our faith.

This chapter is meant to reveal how unbelief comes about. It happens when we listen to the evil report of our sickness, our finances, our sorrows, our worries, our grief, our storms, our obstacles, etc. They are loud and very heavy, but the obstacle of faith's impediment is also meant to reveal how faith is strengthened when we listen to God's word and His promises and allow them to shout above the evil reports.

Noah and Caleb used the whole armor of God and were enabled to lay aside, overcome all the evil reports, overcome all the weights that could have become faith's impediment and hindered their faith journey. We, too, as God's soldiers can follow their example and run our race with patience or endurance. As we daily go to war with our whole armor, we will lay aside all obstacles of discouragement that could be impediments to our faith. We run our race with our eyes focused on the finish line and receive our promise. No impediment here!

Chapter 14

Obstacle: Faith's Journey

He that overcometh shall inherit all things; and I will be
his God, and he shall be my son (Revelation 21:7).

THIS CHAPTER WILL SUM up *Faith's Journey Confronts
Obstacles*. What we must understand is that all of faith's journey
can be an obstacle. It is not overcoming an obstacle and then
smooth sailing. We are in a warfare against spiritual wickedness
that will not be gone until Christ returns. That's why it cannot be
overstated how necessary the armor of God is for God's soldiers.

Before we take another look at the armor of God, let's look at
the scripture reference in Revelation. It reveals why it is imperative
for God's soldiers to overcome by faith. We don't inherit anything
until the end. If we do not overcome, we will not inherit what God
has waiting for His sons and daughters.

> Wherefore come out from among them, and be ye sepa-
> rate, saith the Lord, and touch not the unclean thing; and
> I will receive you, And will be a Father unto you, and ye
> shall be my sons and daughters, saith the Lord Almighty
> (2 Corinthians 6:17–18).

Although God is the Creator of all mankind, He is not the
God of all mankind. This scripture reveals that if we are to be God's

child, we must separate ourselves from all that is contrary to God and all that opposes God. We as God's soldiers cannot allow anything in our life that interferes with our relationship with God. We must understand that unless we overcome, God is not our God. Unless we overcome, we are not going to Heaven. If we live like the world and partake of all its so-called pleasures, God is not our Father.

In chapter one, we learned that unless we become born again through faith's birth, we don't even start on faith's journey. As we went from chapter to chapter, we were shown that faith's journey is a continuous confrontation of obstacles. Of course, the list is probably limitless. However, we have been given an understanding that obstacles can appear anywhere at any time. It is like I revealed in *Storms Are Faith's Workout: Preparing Christians for Spiritual Ambush.* Obstacles like storms are a constant ambush trying to weaken and destroy our faith in God.

God hates sin, and we must abhor that which is evil and cleave to that which is good (Romans 9:9). God's soldiers need to grasp hold of the truth that we cannot overcome in this life if we cleave to sin. It is imperative, essential, and critical to our spiritual life that we recognize evil and loathe it. However, we cannot recognize it if we don't have a knowledge of God's word and know how to use the whole armor of God.

No matter how long that we have been on faith's journey, we must become more proficient in the use of God's armor. There is not time for a sabbatical from our life's warfare. The enemy of our soul is ever watching and ever ready to pounce on us at any time. We are on constant vigil. Yes, there are times that the Lord takes over watching for us when we are asleep (Psalms 4:8), when we are too fatigued from the battles, etc. He will have compassion on us, bind up our wounds, pour in oil and wine, bring us to an inn, and take care of us (Luke 10:30–35).

Let's take another look at the full armor of God. Put on the whole armour of God, that ye may be able to stand against the wiles of the devil (Ephesians 6:10). If we are to overcome all the wiles, the strategies, or the deceitfulness of Satan, we need the whole armor. As I said in chapter four, God's soldiers must not go to war without God's full armor. If we do, the enemy will get the better of us. We will come away looking like the soldiers in my vision or the sons of Sceva.

We are to stand therefore with our loins girt with truth (Ephesians 6:14). That means that we stand erect with God's truth against the lies of the devil. Because we know the truth, we recognize who our enemies are and how they will attack. False doctrines and the enemy's deception are illuminated by the truth of God's word. Along with our loins girt with truth, and the breastplate of righteousness we will defend our heart from wrong affections that could hinder our spiritual life. We will recognize unrighteousness, lies, evil reports, etc. and be able to stand against it. That is why it is vital for God's soldiers to know His word. Without a knowledge of His word, we will not know what is truth or lies. We will not recognize who the false teachers are, and we will be led astray. Without a knowledge of the truth of God's word, our heart will believe the lies, and our spiritual life will be hindered, barren, and fruitless.

The helmet of salvation protects our mind, our thoughts, or what we believe (Ephesians 6:17). Whatever penetrates our mind is what we think about. Without the helmet of salvation, our brain is not protected against thoughts and desires that influence our thinking. Wrong thoughts could sway us to believe lies, false teachers, evil reports, etc. We must always weigh what tries to come into our mind against the truth of God's word. If it is contrary to what we know about God's word, God Himself, or God's ability, it must be rejected as poison. A little leaven leaveneth, corrupts, poisons the whole (Galatians 5:9). We must not be deceived into thinking that a little evil communications is fine. No matter how microscopic, it will destroy our good manners, behavior, or morals (1 Corinthians 15:33).

The sword of the Spirit which is the word of God is backed up with our loins girt with truth. More of God's word and His truth, the more powerful our sword becomes. The sword is of the Holy Spirit and His word is sharper than any two-edged sword piercing through any motives or desires of the heart. Once the word illuminates or discerns the intents, purposes, objectives of the fiery darts, it will destroy the snares of the enemy (Hebrews 4:12). When tempted with anything, we need to quote the word as Jesus did when the devil came at Him. As God's soldiers, we must comprehend that when we speak the word of God clothed in the full armor of God, we will cut to pieces the snares of the devil.

The shield of faith is to protect all the armor (Ephesians 6:16). It protects us against the enemy's diabolical, destructive, distressing fiery darts. The darts are quenched by our faith in God, in His word, and in His ability. It is the shield of faith, along with our loins girt with truth, the helmet of salvation protecting our mind from wrong thoughts, the breastplate of righteousness protecting our heart from affections that could hinder our spiritual life, and the sword of the spirit that will protect us against unbelief.

The means by which we do battle is through persevering prayer. As we continue in prayer, we are working together with God to overcome the obstacle that is hindering us. Too many times, God's soldiers will say a quick prayer and then watch television, play a video game, etc. I am not saying that we can't watch television, play games, etc. What I am saying is that prayer must be without ceasing. Therefore, if that thing which we allow takes our mind and heart away from God, it is best to refrain from it. Whatever we are doing must not take our mind off the importance of staying in tune with God. We are in the world, but not of it. We must be like the butterfly and stay heavenly bound and not revert to the caterpillar that is earthly bound.

Let me interject another story here. When pastoring in Arkansas, a woman in the church came to the altar crying and said that her baby was dead in her womb. They were going to the hospital after church to have a cesarean section. I stood there, and heard the Lord tell me, *"Wherefore take unto you the whole armour of God, that ye may be able to withstand in the evil day, and having done all, to stand."* I felt a little shaky but knew what my God was capable of. I placed my hands on her belly and prayed that life would flow through her baby. Now, let me say nothing seemed to happen. To make a long story short, when she had the baby, he was alive and healthy.

It must be understood, I am not a miracle worker. But when God tells you to pray something, you do it. As I was clothed in His armor, I was endowed with the ability of God's strength to stand against the enemy. Now, on the other hand, when my seven-year-old granddaughter was dying, I sought the Lord for her healing. I remembered the times that He had me pray for people to be healed and my heart cried for it then. However, God gave peace that He was taking her home to be with Him. Yes, it was difficult on my flesh, but I stayed in prayer to keep back any impediments that could interfere with my faith in God. Like darts from the devil that tried to say that He healed strangers when you prayed, but He won't heal your granddaughter, etc. It is God who decides when our time is up in this life. We can be proficient in the armor, persevere in prayer, and be able to wield the sword with precision cuts, but we are not the ones who decide that it is not time to go. We are not the giver and taker of life; only God has that power.

I feel to add something here for those of God's soldiers who feel they can't overcome the obstacle that is obstructing their going forward in their faith journey. The devil is a liar and tries to make us think that there's no way to overcome this habit, addiction, debt, sickness, sin, etc., there's no way God will forgive again for the same sin, there's no way that God truly loves unconditional, etc. The fact that the devil is throwing these lies at us should make us rejoice. He is incapable of telling the truth, so whatever he is saying is opposite of the truth.

This is the time to stand in the whole armor of God and proclaim His word and wield our sword to cut in pieces the devil's fiery darts of lies. Stand firm and quote scripture. *I can do all things through Christ which strengtheneth me* (Philippians 4:13). *For with God nothing shall be impossible* (Luke 1:37). That's why it is imperative that God's soldiers are knowledgeable in the scriptures if we are going to have the wherewith to answer him that reproacheth us, for we trust in His word (Psalms 119:42).

Faith's Journey Confronts Obstacles: Instructing God's Soldiers to Overcome in His Armor is not only meant to give us an awareness that faith's journey is one of lifelong obstacles, but to train, to teach, and to instruct God's soldiers in the use of God's armor. We must remember at all times that the armor is needed for us to overcome by faith. The overcoming involves conquering our flesh or self-will, the world with its enticements, and an enemy who not only hates us but wants to destroy our faith and kill us.

God's soldiers are to be clothed in His full armor at all times. We must always be ready to stand by faith against the evil day. As we stand unshakeable in His armor, we will overcome by faith whatever obstacles the devil puts in our way. The key to staying clothed in the armor is to love God with all our heart, with all our soul, with all our mind, not wavering in our faith, taking up our cross daily, denying ourselves, reading our Bible, praying without ceasing, etc. As we do that, we will become more skillful in the use of the whole armor of God, and we will overcome Satan's obstacles.

My prayer for God's soldiers who have read through to the end of this book is that an understanding of the armor of God has been revealed. It will take time to be fully proficient in its use, but the difference in faith's journey becoming one of victory and not one of defeat will be experienced almost immediately.

What I mean by that is that as I started to learn each piece, I was able to understand where I was lacking in its use. It was like my vision of the defeated soldiers, and I knew that I was losing a battle. Immediately, I pray and ask the Holy Spirit to help me to see where I am spiritually unclothed. It takes time to get out of self and learn to discern which part of the armor is missing or being neglected. I can perceive that I am thinking something contrary to God and His will. I can perceive that I've allowed my affections to be contrary to God and His will. I can perceive that it is not balanced by scriptures. I can perceive that I'm allowing doubt because of the long wait for the promise. I can perceive that I have become weary and not praying without ceasing.

God's soldiers must take seriously the armor, for it is the means to overcome the obstacles and not have them obstruct faith's journey. As we learn what each component does, we will use it with all confidence, stand unshakeable, and overcome. God's soldiers will win battle after battle on faith's journey as we confront every obstacle and overcome in His supernatural armor!

www.ingramcontent.com/pod-product-compliance
Lightning Source LLC
Chambersburg PA
CBHW070507090426
42735CB00012B/2690